A SONG
TO SING,
A LIFE
TO LIVE

A SONG TO SING, A LIFE TO LIVE

Reflections on Music as Spiritual Practice

Don Saliers and Emily Saliers

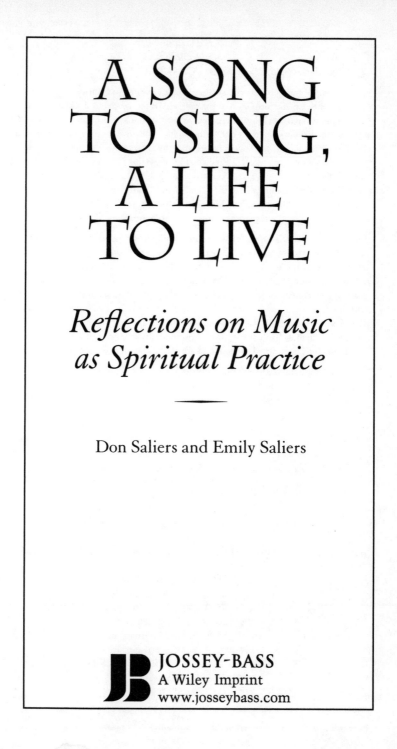
JOSSEY-BASS
A Wiley Imprint
www.josseybass.com

Published by Jossey-Bass
A Wiley Imprint
989 Market Street, San Francisco, CA 94103-1741   www.josseybass.com

Limit of Liability/Disclaimer of Warranty: While the publisher and author have used their best efforts in preparing this book, they make no representations or warranties with respect to the accuracy or completeness of the contents of this book and specifically disclaim any implied warranties of merchantability or fitness for a particular purpose. No warranty may be created or extended by sales representatives or written sales materials. The advice and strategies contained herein may not be suitable for your situation. You should consult with a professional where appropriate. Neither the publisher nor author shall be liable for any loss of profit or any other commercial damages, including but not limited to special, incidental, consequential, or other damages.

Readers should be aware that Internet Web sites offered as citations and/or sources for further information may have changed or disappeared between the time this was written and when it is read.

Credits are on page 209.

Jossey-Bass books and products are available through most bookstores. To contact Jossey-Bass directly call our Customer Care Department within the U.S. at 800-956-7739, outside the U.S. at 317-572-3986, or fax 317-572-4002.

Jossey-Bass also publishes its books in a variety of electronic formats. Some content that appears in print may not be available in electronic books.

Library of Congress Cataloging-in-Publication Data
Saliers, Don E., date.
A song to sing, a life to live: reflections on music as spiritual practice / Don Saliers, Emily Saliers.—1st ed.
p. cm.—(The practices of faith series)
Includes bibliographical references and index.
ISBN-13: 978–0–7879–6717–8 (alk. paper)
ISBN-10: 0–7879–6717–8 (alk. paper)
ISBN-13: 978–0–7879–8377–2 (paperback)
ISBN-10: 0–7879–8377–2 (paperback)
1. Music—Religious aspects. 2. Music—Social aspects. I. Saliers, Emily, date.
II. Title. III. Series.
ML3921.S17 2004
246'.75—dc22

Printed in the United States of America
FIRST EDITION
PB Printing   10 9 8 7 6 5 4 3 2

The Practices of Faith Series
Dorothy C. Bass, Series Editor

———

Practicing Our Faith:
A Way of Life for a Searching People
Dorothy C. Bass, Editor

Receiving the Day:
Christian Practices for Opening the Gift of Time
Dorothy C. Bass

Honoring the Body:
Meditations on a Christian Practice
Stephanie Paulsell

Testimony:
Talking Ourselves into Being Christian
Thomas G. Long

A Song to Sing, A Life to Live:
Reflections on Music as Spiritual Practice
Don Saliers, Emily Saliers

In memory of Carrie,
whose song was loving and fierce

Contents

Editor's Foreword

———

Last Saturday night I went to an Indigo Girls concert for the first time. Even though I have loved their recordings for years, I was not prepared for how powerful this live musical experience would be. Emily Saliers and Amy Ray stood alone on the stage, each with a stringed instrument, and sang while thousands of us in the audience received their gift of sound and responded with our own voices and bodies. We sang along, we danced, and we applauded, saying a heartfelt "yes" to the life-affirming music that encompassed us in that moment.

Near the end of the concert a line from Emily's song "Everything in Its Own Time" latched onto my heart as an expression of how and why this experience was so strong and beautiful. In a world of violence and injustice, the song suggests that "music whispers to you in urgency" and helps you remember "a loving God and things in their own time." How are we to live with hope in this broken world? Here is an answer: "Hold fast to that languageless connection," to the music that urgently whispers the truth.

Each Sunday morning, Don Saliers leads a different community in lamenting the violence and injustice of this world and celebrating the love of God. He does so from the bench of a pipe organ. Here too everyone sings along, and some also dance and applaud. Don often composes a new verse for a familiar tune or a new tune for a familiar verse, and one Sunday morning I was there as he gently and joyfully taught us a fresh song of praise to God. That morning we also sang a hymn I have known for as long as I can remember. As we stood to leave, Don played an intricate, intriguing fugue by Bach that held the community in place for a few minutes longer. In these sounds too I found a languageless connection, a rhythmic, melodious pattern I could hold fast during the coming week, thereby remembering what I had just been told.

In *A Song to Sing, A Life to Live,* Don and Emily help us to see the connections between Saturday night music and Sunday morning music by exploring the spiritual dimensions of music itself. They tell the stories of their own lives in music, and they share what they have learned and observed about the power of music in human life. They help us appreciate the joy of music and also how music carries us into the places of sorrow, where we must go if we are to live with honesty about ourselves and compassion for others.

Along the way Don and Emily cross many boundaries. Their mutual love as father and daughter helps them cross a major division—the musical boundary between generations. Their shared passion for justice leads them across boundaries of nation and culture to embrace music born in experiences of suffering, resistance, and celebration throughout the world. And again and again, they invite us to accompany them across these and other boundaries, remembering the songs of our own lives and finding the courage to join wholeheartedly in the songs of an ever-expanding human community.

I am delighted to add this profound and moving book to the Practices of Faith series, which exists to offer wisdom drawn from deep wells of belief and experience to those who long to live with integrity in the rapidly changing world of the twenty-first century. Each book in the series explores one aspect of human life and asks how it might be lived in a way that reflects the gracious love at the heart of all that is. Most of the authors have written from an explicitly Christian point of view, emphasizing the ways in which each practice has taken shape within the Christian community over time. This book, however, considers music as a "spiritual" practice, thus embracing Don's deep immersion in the life of Christian faith *and* Emily's experience as a person of faith who continues to question organized religion.

I believe that churchgoers and spiritual seekers—and the many persons who are both of these at one time or another—will recognize their own lives and concerns in these pages. And I pray that when this happens they will also reach out to one another, crossing over divisions of generation and style and culture to *listen* with open ears to the many kinds of music that rise up from the passionate, embodied life of humankind.

September 2004   DOROTHY C. BASS
Valparaiso, Indiana   Editor, Practices of Faith Series

Preface

We live in a music-saturated culture. Music is everywhere we go—restaurants, shopping malls, supermarkets, elevators—and many people also carry music around with them, plugging in to portable CD and MP3 players and iPods at every opportunity. Televisions and radios channel more sound into our space, much of it in the form of commercials. Americans go to rock concerts by the thousands, buy records by the millions, and download music from the Internet in unknown numbers. Some people gather to sing together, usually in churches, synagogues, and schools; and some attend recitals and concerts of classical music. Whether we listen by choice or by default, and whatever our musical taste, there's no escaping music in contemporary America.

Yet sometimes music seems so pervasive that we fail to notice how very important music is in giving expression to human life and shaping how each person and community will live. It has become easy to forget that music deepens and makes more vivid the beauty, the delight, and yes, even the lamentable terrors and sufferings of our world. Music is rooted in the human body and the human soul, and it gives voice to the spirit of human communities. Without songs to sing, life would be diminished. Thus, listening to music with care, creating music, sharing music with loved ones or strangers, and developing musical skills are more than ways of making sound.

They are spiritual practices, shared activities open to those who seek lives of greater depth and richness.

This book begins with our firm conviction that music and life are interwoven. We write as a daughter and a father who love a wide range of music. Both of us are practicing musicians, though with very different training and experiences. Each of us has known echoes of a transcendent reality in and through music. Now we want to spend some time together with you in reflecting on the *what,* the *how,* and the *why* of music, especially as music becomes an aspect of human spirituality.

During the past few years, we have had a series of long conversations, learning from one another what it means to make music and to listen deeply to music, sharing with one another our sense of music as a spiritual practice. In the process we found ourselves tracing our musical DNA and thinking about what we desire to share with others in and through our music, as well as about what we reject or seek to overcome as abuses of music. To our surprise the more we shared with one another, the more we found ourselves thinking about questions of faith and spirituality. This is the lens through which we invite you to view music and song in this book.

Emily writes:

> I have spent more than twenty years of my life as a singer-songwriter. My singing partner, Amy Ray, and I have toured extensively as the Indigo Girls, creating what some call alternative folk-rock. Our travels have opened so much of the world to us, seeing and hearing it through music—we have been all over North America,

Europe, Australia, and the Caribbean, as well as parts of Latin America. In all these sometimes wildly different places, I have witnessed how music brings healing to people alienated and broken by attitudes toward sexuality, by political struggles, and by crushing abuses of power. I also have experienced the profound spirituality of music in so-called secular settings. My father, on the other hand, has worked principally in sacred music traditions, while also holding a long-standing interest and talent in jazz and chamber music. As we have talked with each other about music and what it means in our lives, what has emerged from our conversations is a strong sense of crossover and convergence in our views of how music shapes the spiritual searching of each of us.

Don writes:

I have spent nearly fifty years of my life as a keyboard player, cantor, and church musician. My musical compositions and arrangements, unlike Emily's, are intended for church congregations. They aren't earthshaking, but they are important to the worship of my community. Psalms, canticles, anthems, organ improvisations, ritual song—that's the stuff of my work. I too have seen how music can heal the brokenhearted and the alienated. So when Emily and I began to hold the conversations that shaped this book, the crossovers in our experience struck me. At the same time, I was also aware of where we differed as musicians and as listeners. That's what has made writing this book so interesting to me.

These pages have grown out of a conversation that bridges two generations, two approaches to faith, and two genres—the music of Saturday night and Sunday morning. As we have talked and written, each of us has challenged the other's assumptions. What music is secular, and what is sacred? When, if ever, can we say that music is good or bad? We have had to rethink many of our own convictions and revisit many of our diverse experiences. Together we hope that our reflections will prompt in you not simply interesting thoughts but also fresh insights and new intentions. We also hope that they will lead you to embrace new practices in your own life with music.

This book is for anyone who once took piano lessons and wishes now they hadn't quit. It is for those who sing with their communities of faith but who are confused by secular music, and it is for those outside faith communities who wonder whether there is anything true in the songs of organized faith traditions. It is also for anyone who has sung around a campfire, tried to play the French horn, or been captivated by African or Asian drumming. This book is our *yes* to your musical memories and to your musical future. We offer it as an invitation to embrace a broader, deeper vision of the power and role of music in human life—and especially to embrace the spiritual and religious dimensions of attentive listening, collaborative music making, and honest sharing. Such an invitation, we are convinced, is in the long run part of the search for God.

Music is a deep joy, but it also takes work and requires discipline, both in creating and in listening. Music and song bring pleasure, but they also ask something of our minds and hearts. To care for music is very much like caring for other human beings. This is why we can never take music for granted. Each of us has come to understand this in our own way. Every musician who strives for excellence desires listeners with good ears. And every writer desires good readers. Welcome to our conversation.

September 2004
Atlanta, Georgia

Don Saliers
Emily Saliers

Acknowledgments

"The shattering experience of music has been a challenge to my thinking on ultimate issues." This quotation from the great Rabbi Abraham Heschel speaks to our hearts as we finish this book. Grateful for the sheer gift of such a wide range of music and musicians who have shaped our lives and our words and with whom we are privileged to work, we must say thanks. For conversations with Alice Parker and members of the music department at Emory University, for the legacy of Maestro Robert Shaw, for sung prayer at St. John's Abbey in Minnesota, thanks. For Joni Mitchell, Joan Baez, and all the musical influences on us both, thanks. For all the friendships woven into these pages in one way or another, we are deeply indebted, especially for Emily's musical partners and for Don's companions in church music and classroom. Saturday night and Sunday morning music making with talented friends and attentive listeners—all of these are present in our conversations before, beneath, and beyond the text.

This book owes a great deal to the keen and generous editorial work of Dorothy Bass, director of the Valparaiso Project on the Education and Formation of People in Faith, a Lilly Endowment project that supported the writing of this book. Susan Briehl and Don Richter researched and wrote the References section.

Thanks also to our many other colleagues who worked together on *Practicing Our Faith: A Way of Life for a Searching People* (Jossey-Bass, 1997) and *Way to Live: Christian Practices for Teens* (Upper Room, 2002). To those lively souls we owe the genesis and spirit of our collaborative effort. Sincere thanks to Guy and Candie Carawan, from whom we have learned so much about music and justice in America. Special thanks go to Mary Catherine Foster, a student at Candler School of Theology, for assistance with early manuscript work; to Susan Henry Crowe, dean of religious life at Emory University, for valuable comments at crucial points in the process; and to Sue Witty, who faithfully produced typescripts of thirty hours of our conversations before we started writing the book. Gratitude in special measure to Emily's life partner, Leslie Zweben, whose support and lovely sensibility have sustained Emily through the process, and to Jane Saliers, matrix, monitor, and storytelling witness of a sometimes wild musical household.

D. S.
E. S.

A SONG
TO SING,
A LIFE
TO LIVE

Chapter 1

TRACING OUR SONGLINES

———

Imagine that you were given a song when you were born. Suppose that as you grew into childhood, your grandparents taught you how to listen for music that connected you to your ancestors. But suppose as well that your future pathways in life were discovered over time as you traced that music and learned to improvise on your song. Human communities have, from the beginning of time, explored identity and destiny in music and song. Such "songlines," as these may be called, link generation to generation. This image has captivated our imagination as we write about the mystery and power of music in our lives.

In this book we are tracing songlines as well. Music making seems to be in our family DNA, laying down a pathway from generation to generation. Coming alive to music is coming alive to deep memory, as music re-creates our sense of the world and who we are in it, right in the midst of the terrors and beauties, the pain and deep pleasures, of human existence. Coming alive to music, we are led on a double journey: into the mystery of God and into the depths of our humanity. If we listen well, we may even hear the voices of ancestors and of cultures and communities we've never met.

Music can make us come alive, provided that we bring our lives to the music. For each of us, life and music intertwine. Without songs and music making, neither one of us could understand the stories of our particular lives. And without songs and music making, neither of us could understand what words like *spirit* and *spirituality* mean either. For us music and song are intimately related to spirituality, to being alive to what is deepest in and about the human journey.

Early in the process of writing this book, we interviewed one another. Listening to what music has brought each of us and where it has taken us as individual musicians was a revelatory experience for us as daughter and father. We learned things we had not known about one another. We also became aware of questions about the future, because looking back in time also means leaning forward toward what has not yet been. "Well, I don't know where it all began," the Indigo Girls sing in a recent song, "and I don't know where it all will end." Where to begin? Where to end? We'll trace our songlines first with Emily, and then with Don, and then back another generation to Don's own father.

Emily's Story

At some level I always knew that a life of music was waiting for me, that it came down to me through all the gen-

A Song to Sing, A Life to Live

erations before me. When I was nine years old, my teacher passed out a flyer advertising various activities at the local YMCA. I remember holding the brightly colored sheet in my hand, looking at the listing for guitar lessons, and feeling a flush of excitement and inevitability—I was going to play guitar. After I got permission from my mom and dad, my cousin Kevin (who was at the time a professional singer-songwriter) took me to pick out a $24 nylon string guitar. From that day on, I played. There was no other path.

Coming into the gift of music is a rare privilege, one that I have never taken for granted a single day of my life. Music has given and still gives me everything: a working partner in Amy Ray, who to this day still inspires me with her burning gift; experiences with and stories of countless communities we as the Indigo Girls have encountered through our travels and their spirit of perseverance even in challenging and deadly times; and along the way, brilliant mentors like the justly acclaimed Native American activist Winona Laduke and former U.S. president Jimmy Carter, to name just two. I have had the privilege of witnessing and taking part in the great healing power of song, especially communal song as audience and performers become one. I've seen people whose souls seemed homeless find a home and a family in particular songs that called their name. For me music has fleshed out the beautiful and the ugly, one and the same, both equally important.

When Dorothy Bass asked me to write this book with my dad, and I realized it was going to have religious connections and connotations, I felt great fear. I have been deeply disappointed in the organized church and other organized religions, particularly in the way they treat anyone who is queer and in the brutal legacy of church missions for indigenous peoples, especially Native Americans. I am appalled at the devastation and enormous injustice that have been inflicted in the name of God. How many people all over the world over long centuries have been killed in Christ's name? How many have the church and other organized religions ostracized for one reason or another? How many church people are now suddenly aware of the history of sexual abuse? I will never turn away from this darkness, and I respect the pain of those who have been hurt by religion. And yet . . .

Although I do not identify solely with one faith and am truly a religious "mutt," I grew up going to church and being raised as a person of faith. I have seen how genuine faith was at the heart of the civil rights movement in America and how faith that works for justice can change the course of history. My faith is deeply personal and not something easily articulated. But faith in the Creator and Sustainer of all things is my reason for being. Music and faith are, for me, intimately related, even as I continue to wrestle with questions about organized religion.

Writing this book has led me to ask once again: What is secular, and what is sacred? Singing in church choirs as a very young girl, I was introduced to the woven harmonies and canons and counterpoints that directly influenced my folk music arrangements later on. The tremendous power and poetry of biblical images have landed comfortably in many an Indigo Girls song. I have felt the intensity of sacred music not only in the hallowed halls of church but also in the smoky bars of Atlanta, where all the "freaky people" (as musician Michael Franti says) gather night after night to sing together, prop each other up through tragedy and joy, and cry an implicit prayer with all their hearts. One place smells of incense and candles, the other of cigarette smoke and beer. I can't say one experience is more deeply spiritual than the other.

Saturday night morphs into Sunday morning as I sit down with my father and we talk about how those two days and two ways are not really so separate. We speak of how music can deepen human life beyond measure and bring us closer to the truth of what it means to be human and to the transcendent power of love beyond our understanding. Music, we keep saying, is some kind of mysterious mediator between us and the God we seek.

DON'S STORY

My songlines come from the mixture of classical and jazz streams flowing through my father, his sister, our church, and my school. Early on I was exposed to a whole range of church music, and with early keyboard lessons came good sight-reading skills. This meant that I was called upon to play hymns and accompany singers in church and in school and soon had a reputation as the town accompanist. Then came violin and clarinet. High school was filled with musical commitments: choir, orchestra, band, chamber groups, operettas, and by tenth grade, my first jazz trio. Making music, I also learned to listen. I still remember a regional orchestral rehearsal where a sophomore oboe player from Toledo played what at the time seemed the sweetest most ravishing passage I had ever heard. I can still hear that sound.

I remember playing Gershwin's "Rhapsody in Blue" with a community orchestra when I was thirteen. That remains a kind of epiphany. I knew that I had accomplished something after long practice. My father, still at that time struggling with alcoholism, recognized that I was doing well, and he was able to tell me so. Later, as a piano major in college, I performed Bach's partitas on the keyboard, while also playing with a jazz quintet and making some money with various pickup bands. I loved it that Dad heard my senior recital.

It is hard for me to say much about my own early development, musically and spiritually, without saying more about my dad. My father was an alcoholic; and it was music that took him to, through, and finally away from the bottle. He met my mother, Emilie, Austrian by birth, in New York. She was a dancer, and he was a jazzman, living the life of the mid-1920s. She was beautiful and talented, and he was dashing. Fading pictures at the Astor Hotel and other venues show them, twenty-somethings, in the Big Apple, daring and vivacious. He played alto and tenor sax, clarinet, violin, and guitar and sang with a stand-up jazz band of the period. Dad would tell me about finishing gigs in midtown and then driving up to Harlem for what he called the "real sessions." The Harlem Renaissance was in full swing. What music makers were there! Willie "the Lion" Smith, Meade "Lux" Lewis, Albert Ammonds, players from the Apollo Theatre, and later a young blind piano player from Toledo named Art Tatum. The spirit of that incredible time got into my bloodstream. Alongside my early classical piano training, I would listen to the old 78 rpm vinyl recordings and best of all, learn some of the jazz styles from music books purchased from Ernie Duffield's Music Store.

Later Dad would tell me tales of how the high life was too much. Like the night he fell down a flight of stairs in New York on top of his cherished violin, smashing it beyond repair. High talent, high octane, high life, and then the Great Depression. I was born in small-town Ohio after he had hit the skids and returned to find some kind of employment. In the midst of their struggles, my mother was diagnosed very late with cancer. She died in 1942, when I was not yet five. That's how it was that I went to live with my father's sister, Alice, who provided me with a good home and lots of musical encouragement. She was a soprano and a church choir director. So it was piano lessons from an early age and gradually more and more exposure to choir practice and Sunday mornings at the local Methodist church. She and my uncle held steady while my father struggled on with factory work, teaching music lessons and playing in the local Veterans of Foreign Wars marching band during sober times.

In the midst of the struggle, music came to his rescue. A local Methodist pastor decided that he would like to form a Sunday school orchestra for the church, and he had just the person in mind to direct it. So it was that my father, reluctantly at first, took this on. It was a funny little clutch of players, but it gave him a new venue for music making and a new image among some of the town folk who only knew him as the musically gifted drunk, not an angry drunk but a sentimental one. At the same time, one or two of his musical buddies and others were able to persuade him to try Alcoholics Anonymous. That's not a story for now, but it is important to say that in my early teenage years I received my father back. To this day I attribute much of his recovery to that odd little Sunday school orchestra, with his lead violin waving to give us the tempo. In his recovered life, he formed a dance band that eventually had quite a reputation around northwest Ohio. That, together with his ability to teach a range of instruments, gave him a rich musical life. It wasn't New York, but he was very good again. So I came to treasure his legacy.

I will never forget when I began to play now and then with his dance band around 1953. His style was easy; and he usually played the popular songs of the day, many in his own arrangements, somewhat in the manner of Guy Lombardo. As for me, I was always listening to jazz—the late Art Tatum, the early Dave Brubeck, the emerging Gerry Mulligan, Stan Kenton, Miles Davis, and company. Can you imagine the first time I took a piano solo against the melodious dance music and ventured with a set of wild Brubeckian block chords? Dad, who had already heard enough of Stan Kenton to know that was not his kind of music, said to me during the break, "Son, can you keep the progressive stuff down?" That was one side of our musical relationship. The other was accompanying his violin or clarinet students—sometimes he would play an entire piece for them himself, with me at the keyboard—and my own wonderful Sunday afternoon lessons with him. A high

A SONG TO SING, A LIFE TO LIVE

point was the Bach Double Violin Concerto—especially the slow movement—what an afternoon it was when I could finally play through the whole movement without stopping! Those collaborations are, for me now, long after his death, deep life-giving images. Whenever I hear some of the music we did together, it all comes back. That's what music does—it encodes life, most especially shared life. You don't have to be a performer to know this, but if you have ever done music together with someone, you know this with special intensity.

When my father shared his passion for both jazz and classical music with me, he opened up a world for me and also opened up his life—a life of pain, tumult, and joy—leaving me finally with a deep sense of connection. I have a scratchy old 78 rpm vinyl, recorded in 1929, of his tune, "Better Keep Away from Me," and also his sketchbooks of his arrangements of standards from the 1920s through the early 1950s. Recently, as I sorted through some closet shelves, a folder of music paper fell out. There, in his own notation, were several arrangements of Christmas carols, first sketched for that little church band years ago. When I sit down to play from these books or listen to that old record, Emily's grandpa is very present. I am very grateful. He lives in the music. And the music sounds in this air, here and now. Music draws me into this mystery.

So it was music that took our forebear to many places. For him music making opened up several worlds, including one that he shared with Emily and her three sisters and with me. Our visits to him in Port Charlotte, Florida, where he retired, always included making music together. He also directed a Methodist church choir and the community chorus during these years. I will never forget him, at age seventy-six, responding to my question about how the choirs were doing. He blurted out, "It would be OK except for these damn stubborn old people!" So much for gentle opinions. But his choirs did well. Despite his short fuse and quick retorts, he gave the singers his passion and his feel for the music.

By the way, he lived long enough to know that Emily had promising talent on the guitar and in singing. He tried to get her interested in his kind of music (just as he had done with me thirty years before), telling her to listen to the Quintet from the Hot Club of France. But at age fifteen, Emily would be moving in a different direction. Just as my first piano breaks with his band headed out at another angle, so Emily's early song writing traced a different line.

One day we had been speaking of Emily's grandfather when she commented:

> I remember when I was first impressed with your music, Dad. When I came into that little church in New Haven and first heard and saw you playing the organ. I thought: *How can he play with both hands and his feet too?* The music just rolled over me; it was Bach of course—one of his great fugues. Later I was amazed to learn that you collaborated in writing a musical takeoff of Shakespeare's *Hamlet,* a production called *Elsinore.* I was old enough to know it was pretty daring, . . . and I can still sing the opening theme, "There's going to be a wedding at Elsinore. They'll have to change the bedding . . . at Elsinore!" But now I

realize that you, like my grandfather, are equally at home in jazz and classical music.

I remember Emily too, of course. I remember going with her to her guitar lessons on Saturday mornings in Atlanta. She was learning to play some of the classical literature, Fernando Sor, but also the Beatles' "Blackbird" and others. But then one morning I heard her play a song about pollution and people not caring, and I knew she had the gift to cross over.

SEEKING AND SPEAKING THE LANGUAGE OF THE SOUL

In all these ways and more, we have received our songlines—musical legacies that are deeply spiritual—and also claimed the freedom to improvise within those legacies. Some people inherit musical talent and training directly from parents or relatives—it seems to be in the genes. Many great musicians come from musical families. But others are inspired by strangers, just by listening to a singer or to a well-played violin, trumpet, or piano. Most people, some of whom can't carry a tune in a bucket, do not inherit a gift for playing music. But in church or in school or simply with a group of friends, the sound of people singing creates a yearning to sing along. This is the beginning of coming alive to the richer and more interesting world that emerges when we know and love music.

Our songlines have helped each of us to cross over into the music of another generation. This is something that seems difficult for many people today. But we who do so find ourselves opening our ears and our senses to what is new. This does not mean that we must like the other's music, but it does mean that we should try to attend to the music and to the person, always seeking to discover whatever is excellent and profoundly human enough to touch another's heart. Doing so, we open our vulnerabilities and our hearts to people "other" than ourselves, asking, What music touches down in them? And has some of this music journeyed across time, gathering experience from another generation than our own?

One of our deepest hopes in writing this book is to encourage readers to practice this kind of appreciative crossing over into music that is not immediately their own, not only across generations but also across other lines of culture, ethnicity, race, and class. We hope that our stories will encourage you to listen for whatever is excellent or profoundly human in another's music.

Similarly, we hope that our reflections here will encourage readers to treat others' spirituality with respect and openness, and we believe that sharing our experiences and thoughts about music across the lines that often divide people can help this to happen. Because everything in life can be touched in music, we think music could be conceived as a primary soul practice. It is in the very nature of music to awaken our souls to matters beyond the ordinary. Whether we are listening alone or together, performing from a score or improvising, sharing our responses, or just pondering what we have heard, the

A SONG TO SING, A LIFE TO LIVE

practices of music engage us at a very deep level. Such powerful engagement is not always used for good, to be sure: music can be used for propaganda, nationalism, sexism, and cruelty. Yet it can also bring us to the animating center of life. This is why many call music the language of the soul made audible.

Emily speaks of how the communion song "Let Us Break Bread Together" always gets to her at some deep level.

> The images in that song tear me apart: "When I fall on my knees with my face to the rising sun, O Lord, have mercy on me." I think of how this world and all of us need mercy. We are fallible creatures. "Have mercy on me" is a cry of the heart and soul. And when I sing this with a gathered community of vulnerable people who really wish to share the bread and wine of life's table and hope to live a life of truth and grace, the music goes right to my soul.

And the song concludes by inviting lifelong praise because of the mercy and release.

Don recalls sitting beside his grandmother in church as a child.

> The old Methodist church pews were hard wood, and the worship service seemed long and boring. But when the hymns were sung, I would stand beside her, hearing her quavering voice, and try to sing with the rest, "Holy, holy, holy . . . early in the morning our song shall rise to Thee." That hymn is imprinted in my body and soul. I did not

realize at the time that I was actually addressing the God of all creation in the very words of the seraphim, those strange angelic beings described in Isaiah's vision of the heavenly court of God (Isaiah 6). Nor did I realize then that I would someday come to understand that holiness and awe before God had everything to do with how life might be lived. I suspect now that my work as a musician and as a theologian owes more to that familiar hymn than I can quite comprehend.

Through the singing practices of our religious communities, each of us has received spiritual gifts. When a religious community sings of its great need for mercy or shares hymns expressing thanksgiving and awe, something is given to each soul, something that is then released into the world's life stream. But of course, this does not happen only in church. Emily points to the remarkable song *"Gracias a la Vida,"* by the Chilean singer Violeta Parra. As we listened to this song together, we realized that both the music and the words spoke what we often long to say in response to the gift of life.

Gracias a la vida que me ha dado tanto.	Thanks to life, which has given me so much.
Me dió dos luceros que cuando los abro	It gave me two morning stars, which, when I open them,
perfecto distingo lo negro del blanco	I clearly distinguish black from white
y en el alto cielo su fondo estrellado	and high in the sky its starry depths
y en las multitude el hombre que yo amo.	and from the crowds the man I love.

After this expression of gratitude for vision, the song speaks next of the gift of hearing, of the night crickets and canaries, of barking dogs and dark clouds and the tender voice of the beloved. "Gracias a la Vida" echoes again and again throughout the song. Gratitude for "el sonido y el abedecedario" (the sound and the alphabet) with words to think and speak, for "mother," "friend," "brother," and the "light that brightens the path of the soul of my loved one." And finally:

Gracias a la vida que
   me ha dado tanto.
Me ha dado la risa y me had
   dado el llanto,
asi yo distingo dicha de
   quebranto
los dos materials que forman
   mi canto
y el canto de ustedes que es
   el mismo canto
y el canto de todos que es
   mi propio canto.

Thanks to life, which has
   given me so much.
It has given me laughter
   and has given me tears
so that I distinguish
   between joy and loss,
the two components of
   my song
and your song, which are
   one and the same,
and everyone's song,
   which is my own song.

This exquisite love song does not mention God. But listening to it, Don was filled with the sense that the gratitude expressed here is very close to the thanksgiving expressed in the authentic prayers of people of faith. Then Emily mentioned that Violeta Parra had taken her own life. And we both pondered the mystery: Out of what complex turmoil did this luminous lyric of thanks come? When words and music touch those chords in us, we must take notice. The point is not to categorize music as secular or sacred; the point is to notice that we are in the presence of a human soul and to listen with care and respect from the depths of our own souls.

In his spiritual autobiography, *Dancing Madly Backwards,* Paul Marechal tells of a dark night when a verse of a psalm he had sung in compline (an evening prayer service) "began to move around inside me, like the Spanish *canto hondo*—deep song. I found myself cooperating with this music, leaning into it, knowing that when its last note vanished into the silence, another leaf would be living on the tree I call 'myself.'" *Canto hondo,* deep song, is what can shape authentic spirituality. The language of the soul becomes audible in such song. We should always be on the search for it, within a worshiping community or wherever it appears.

WALKING THE SONGLINES OF FAITH

For both of us, certain music from the Christian tradition has shaped our art. It is another songline. However, it is one that always leads to paradox. The more one learns to express awe and thanks and to cry out for mercy to God, the more one is plunged into the depths of what it is to be human. At the same time, the more one sounds the depths of human experience, the more one finds the mystery of God unfolding. This paradox is not just a religious cliché but rather something both of us keep discovering right in the midst of our making, listening, hearing, sharing, and struggling to make sense of music, our own and that of others.

Don recalls the great orchestra and choral conductor Robert Shaw saying again and again that great art and good music required two things: awareness of human suffering and a sense of mystery. As many who have worked with him know, Shaw was not a pious man. In many ways he was always in reaction against the clichés of religious piety; this preacher's kid had experienced more than enough of church. Nevertheless, his performances of works such as Brahms's *German Requiem* or Mahler's *Das Lied von der Erde* ("Song of the Earth") could be absolutely transcendent experiences in the concert hall, evoking so much more than most church musicians could hope for. In each year's annual Christmas concerts with the Atlanta Symphony Orchestra and Chorus, Don was always stunned when Shaw would suddenly whirl around on the podium and proclaim with fiery intensity the Magnificat, the prophetic song of Jesus' mother upon learning that she would bear a child (Luke 1:46–53). This was especially powerful when it followed Wendell Whalem's arrangement of *"Bethelehememu,"* an African burst of praise to God for becoming human in Jesus the Christ, sung to polyrhythmic drumbeats by the renowned African American men's singing group, the Morehouse College Glee Club.

Because music is so close to human emotion and feeling, and because faith is a matter of both the head and the heart, it leads us again and again into the realm of spirituality. As Emily observes, "Anyone who struggles with love and suffering and searches for the mystery ends up singing—or at least listening to music." This is because music engages these things like nothing else does, evoking questions even when we find it hard to find answers. Yet sometimes music does lead to assurance. Don has heard many church people confess that it is easier for them to believe certain things when they sing them instead of just saying them, much less try to explain them. These mysteries are the essence of religious belief and life.

Music helps us enter our humanity more fully, by embracing the most mysterious things about us and about our lives in time and space. For the two of us, as we hope for you who read the pages to follow, the task is to open all of our lives to the mystery and depth of being alive, to lay aside our initial prejudices and our well-formed responses and to listen, really listen. Doing this, we begin to understand why religious faith requires music. It is a matter of connecting and reconnecting to the most elemental senses of life—to beauty, sorrow, joy, hope, and gratitude.

Chapter 2

A SOUND SPIRITUALITY

———

W hen Emily was fourteen, our family lived for a year near a Benedictine monastery in Collegeville, Minnesota. Emily remembers how the bells of St. John's Abbey Church sounded the rhythm of our days. As they called the monks to worship at particular hours, the great bells also anchored our family to the passage of time. On Sundays and festival days, the bells rang longer riffs over the lakes and trees and countryside, adding texture and rhythm to our family meals and celebrations.

Meanwhile the monks in the abbey were chanting psalms that were first sung and then written down in ancient Hebrew as long as three millennia ago. The Psalms—of which 150 are collected in the Bible—are now treasured by both Jews and Christians. These ancient poem-songs are filled with sound and permeated with images of sound. Psalm 81, for example, begins

> Shout aloud to God our strength:
> shout for joy to the God of Jacob.
> Raise a song, sound the tambourine,
> the sweet lyre with the harp.

19

Blow the trumpet at the new moon,
at the full moon, on our festal day.
—Psalm 81:2–4

And the psalm that traditionally comes last in the Psalter sounds forth with a massive burst of instrumentation, reaching out to include all creation in the music:

Praise! Praise God with trumpet sound,
praise God with lute and harp.
Praise God with tambourine and dance,
with strings and pipes.
Praise God with clanging cymbals;
praise God with loud clashing cymbals!
Let everything that breathes praise the Lord!
—Psalm 150:3–6

Whenever human beings have gathered for worship, prayer, or meditation, music has been there. Certain ordered sounds, our ancestors discovered long ago, awaken and sustain certain states of awareness. Often these sounds communicate specific messages because they are part of ritual gatherings, like the monks' prayers or the ancient Israelites' trumpets. In other traditions as well, ordered sound evokes feelings and captures the attention of communities that are attuned to them. The shofar calls Jews to Shabbat and carries the cries of the people to God; the *kayagam* resonates in Korean tradition; the chant of the muezzin announces the time for prayer in Islam. During our travels the two of us have heard the sound of bells in Hindu and Buddhist temples and the beat of drums in African and Native American

A Song to Sing, A Life to Live

worship. Both Tibetan monasteries and Moravian Christmas celebrations incorporate the loud brightness of brass instruments. The Christian services most familiar to our family are more likely to rely on the sounds of the organ, piano, flute, and strings, and more recently guitar and electronic keyboard. But the most important instrument of all—one that is used in every tradition— is the human voice.

EMBODYING MUSIC— HEART AND SOUL

The human body with all its senses is the primary location of the impulse to acknowledge the glory and power of God. Rituals, whether sacred or secular, always involve the body and its senses—what is heard, seen, tasted, touched, and given bodily expression in movement and gesture. Even those who are spiritual but not religious, as many people describe themselves today, necessarily experience the holy in and through embodied life. Spirituality is not an idea in the brain but rather a disciplined bodily experience that grows deeper with practice. If we are to grasp why and how true spirituality takes root in human beings, we must attend to the power of sound and its impact on us as sensual, sensuous, sensitive beings.

Music begins in our bodies. Our bodies are prepared to hear and respond. Tiny membranes in our ears—our eardrums—vibrate to the sounds that come from outside ourselves. But not only our ears pick up the sounds of music. Think of deaf people who dance, feeling the beat, or of the extraordinary music of Evelyn Glennie, the deaf percussionist who often performs concertos written for her with prominent symphony orchestras. Think of the great German composer Ludwig van Beethoven, who in his later life could not hear his own music and had to listen for vibrations through the floor. Those of us with hearing may not realize that we too are moved in our whole bodies, though we are usually less aware of it than are those with hearing impairment. Because of our bodies' resonance, music that comes from outside ourselves sounds inside us as well.

But our bodies do not only respond to music; they make music. Each person is a bundle of sound. The sounds of our bodies and our mothers' bodies are our first music. We breathe in and out, slowly, rapidly, gently, or in great gulps. A child skips down the sidewalk or marches soldierlike in strict tempo. We walk across a room or toward another person slowly, quickly, sometimes breaking into a run; and as we do, we breathe more rapidly as well. We meet and embrace with racing heartbeat. So the rhythms of our bodies are intimately related to the rhythms of our being in the world. Our heartbeats, our breathing out and in, our cries of delight and pain, and our movements through space and time are already musical, gifted with pulse, pitch, pace, and rhythm. So the music we hear and sing and play has a wondrous sounding board within us. Unless we pay no attention or deliberately suppress our senses, the body is always being touched by music, is always ready to become a musical instrument.

Even before birth the beating heart and pulsing blood we hear in our mothers' wombs gives rhythm to our days. Susan, a dear friend of ours, remarked on how she felt when she first heard the heartbeat of her child in the womb. That rhythm of life was there within her, and yet distinct from her own. When her daughter, Eleanor, had a touch of asthma as a child, Susan would put her ear to Eleanor's chest to listen for her breathing and would hear that same heartbeat again. Thinking back on those early years, Susan now beholds her grown daughter as part of the very music of her life. Their hearts beat quite separately, yet whenever joy or pain or even some misunderstanding reconnects them and draws them into conversation, something of that original primal bonding reappears.

Some musicians deliberately take account of the human heart in creating powerful musical experiences. A few summers ago, Don was teaching at the Vancouver School of Theology in Canada during the weeks when people from several First Nations tribes were there for two weeks of study. Early each morning we gathered in the chapel for a worship service of the Word and the Table. Each morning the assembly would begin with a gathering procession during which the leaders of worship from a particular tribal group would enter to the sound of a drumbeat. Without words they moved to encircle the room and invite us to move with them. The sound of the drum was like a cosmic heartbeat: dum-poom, dum-poom, dum-poom. As the circling moved toward silence, the four directions were honored and the room itself made a holy place. Don remembers, "I found my own heart literally slowing to the beat of the drum and the movement of the procession." The bodily memory of that entrance and the merging of drum and heartbeat have stayed with Don. Sometimes now in other places, the picture of that gathering in a circle of rhythm comes back to him as a vivid image of how humankind can honor the cosmos, a place, and a people.

The human heart beats—slowly, quickly, with intense pounding, or gently—depending on what is happening to us. Those rhythms accompany all our days and become a deep metaphor for how we feel the world. Perhaps that is why songs about love always talk about the heart, from "Don't go breakin' my heart" to "My heart stood still." The body's actual, beating heart becomes a metaphor, generating basic images for what we experience and what we become over time. It is no accident that religious traditions also use the root metaphor of the heart when they wish to speak of the deepest part of human beings, from a Sufi derived chant "listen, listen, listen, to my heart's song" to "hearts unfold like flowers before Thee" in the well-known hymn "Joyful, Joyful, We Adore Thee."

And when we sing this praise, we breathe. Without breath there is no sound, no singing at all. In biblical images, to breathe is to live. The wonderful Hebrew word *ruach* means breath and spirit. *Ruach* is what the Bible says God breathed into human beings at the creation (Genesis 2:7), the breath of life, and the *ruach* of God was also understood to be the inspiration of men and women who speak poetry and proclaim prophecy. The English poet George Herbert speaks of "God's breath in man returning to his birth." This is the root meaning of the word *inspiration*—literally the in-breathing of spirit in the human mind and imagination. There is a deep connection between breathing and singing. It is therefore no wonder—and yet nonetheless a very wondrous thing—that it is breath that allows us to sing. When we are inspired by a song, it is as though the vibrating breath and spirit of the singer enters our own.

Emily and Don have both had good choir experiences along the way. Every good conductor knows that breath support is crucial to making good vocal sound. Emily remembers the first time her high school choir conductor said, "Let your breath pull the line through the whole phrase." And it was a kind of magic. Composer and arranger Alice Parker, who is known for her ability to get ordinary people to sing together, keeps working until the singers learn how to sing whole phrases "on the breath." Good singing requires stamina and breath control, as all solo singers know. We think this is why when we have strong experiences of singing together, we sense a deep connection between the spirit of song and spirituality.

The movements and gestures we make are also musical. Why do babies and small children love to bang on pots and pans? Why do children love hand-clapping games? It is because the rhythms and tones we make this way express our feelings even before we have words. The body provides our first percussion instrument. Suddenly, we are laughing at the wonderful memories of being part of a kindergarten rhythm band, clanging and banging on whatever was available. One professional group of musicians, skilled in a whole range of music, develops this art;

the group's name is Bang on a Can. What begins in our childhood becomes, over time, more complex. We can train our hands and feet to make incredible rhythms. Those of us who play instruments like the piano or the guitar come to actually feel the shape of the chords and the melodies in our hands. Playing the organ, as Don does, required learning to feel the pedal keyboard with legs and feet together. Playing the guitar or banjo, as Emily does, requires the coordination of both hands and fingers. No wonder we can think of music as being in our fingers and arms and legs, in fact, in our whole bodies.

When little Marie (Emily's niece) wants to dance for us, it is clear that she is hearing some inner music to which she moves. Waving hello or good-bye, walking or running toward or away from somebody—all of these have a kind of intrinsic musical quality. When we see people rushing to embrace someone just off the plane at an airport, we can almost hear the body singing. When two people make a last farewell or a child on someone's shoulder waves a very small and slow good-bye, we can almost hear the gesture's sad music.

Watching a group of musicians play together reveals a whole range of gestures, nods, smiles, glances (sometimes glares!), and intakes of breath. Often Emily and Amy lean toward one another, sometimes moving together, when the music calls for intricate passages or simply when they are really in a groove. There are times when the whole band is intensely physically connected. The same thing happens all the time in chamber music. The physical interaction of the members of a string quartet is like a conversation in gesture. In fact, part of the

A Song to Sing, A Life to Live

great joy of hearing excellent musicians perform is in "seeing" the music in and through their nonverbal communication.

Don's friend Mark Burrows brought home to us recently the depth of music's place in the body when he gave a remarkable account of near death and recovery. In the spring of 2002, Mark's brother, John, suffered a sudden liver failure. At the time the physicians and the family were uncertain of the cause of John's illness, but as John slipped away from consciousness, it was clear that he might not survive. The only hope was a liver transplant, which finally came at the very last moment. As John struggled for his life and then slowly emerged from a coma, Mark listened, reflected, and wrote:

> On the surface, amid all the motion surrounding his bed, John lies still and seems to be veiled in an interior silence. He is still unable to speak because of all the tubes inserted down his throat for respiration and feeding, even though he is slowly emerging from the coma into some boundary place of awareness. We wonder, could he speak if this were physically possible? A silence surrounds him, broken only by the slow, steady rhythm of his breathing and the ventilator's machine-hum. But what do we really know of the body's interior sounds? How silent is it at rest? Nurses and doctors listen with stethoscopes from time to time; they hear things hidden from the naked ear, sounds that are always happening: the stirring breath entering lungs as they swell and contract; the deep churnings of the stomach and intestines managing the flow of foods in that slow muscular

pull by which matter is converted into energy; the deep drumbeat of the heart muscle pumping and receiving, pumping and receiving, keeping a steady rhythm of blood flowing out and back from moment to moment. No silence here, though most of this music—if such it is—remains veiled from the ordinary attunement of our ears.

And this is a peculiar learning: that the deep sounds of life, the ones necessary for the body's vital functioning, remain largely unknown to us. We are not conscious of them, cannot manage them, and must trust them with an involuntary obedience, if we can call it that. These sounds honor a logic belonging to some primal memory dwelling in the cells and membranes, the complex web of organs and tissues constituting "the organism." Perhaps they hum quietly, in their own way, as they go about their jobs. Perhaps they groan and cry out under the travail of pain. Perhaps they have their own kind of song. Perhaps they, too, know fear and joy, recognize comfort and danger. We cannot finally know with any certainty; they remain inaudible to us, hidden from our unassisted ear. But they do their "work," if we might call it this, with a dignity we come to know primarily when it is in question, when the body is in crisis. And perhaps, finally, all of this is a music, an intricate orchestration of the many separate parts in order to bring forth a common song.

We include this passage because of how truly it resonates with our experience. With all the differences between the music Emily composes and sings and the music Don makes in church and in recitals, we both sense that we are able to connect to the sounds we take in from outside ourselves because there is something inside our bodies that recognizes and resonates with them.

Music Resounding— Within, Around, Beyond

Music, as we have seen, is so very close to us, lodged deep within our bodies. It is about as down to earth as anything can be. But at the same time, it exists beyond our bodies, connecting us to larger realities. Music is much bigger than we are, pervading the entire universe both in a physical sense and in its transcendent dimensions.

A different friend also named Mark—a man of many interests who is fascinated by religion, music, and science—suggests that music can tell us something about the unity of the universe itself. "Music is not just a human thing," he says. "In some ways it is truly a universal language. To quote the Oscar Hammerstein classic, 'The hills are alive with the sound of music!' But so are the trees and the planets, the rivers and the fields. Indeed, the entire universe is alive with the sound of music!"

Whether you live near the beach or in the center of the city, whether your home is on the hot plains of Texas or in the hills of Tennessee, music is there. Its sounds vary—the crash of surf on the beach, the rumble of buses in the city streets, the electric whirring of cicadas, the rustle of leaves on an autumn day—but rhythm and harmony are everywhere. It's as if the whole of creation is caught up in some fantastic symphony.

Scientists used to think that the smallest particles in the universe were atoms. Then they discovered electrons and protons. Then came quarks. Now scientists have discovered something they call strings. These are like tiny pieces of spaghetti, except millions of times smaller. They vibrate just like strings on a violin or guitar but at a fantastically high frequency. If the scientists are right, that means that the most fundamental particle in the universe is a vibrating string. Think of it! This offers a new way of understanding a very old idea: the whole creation is singing to God.

Christians and Jews tell the story of God speaking everything into existence (see the first chapter in the Bible). But there is something quite harmonious and musical about the way creation responds to God's voice. The biblical vision of the world is full of music. "O sing to the Lord a new song; sing to the Lord, all the earth!" (Psalm 96:1). It's as if all of creation can't help but sing out God's praise. The floods clap their hands; the hills sing for joy (Psalm 98:8).

Different peoples have different ways of understanding this music that runs throughout creation. In an ancient sacred story from India, a deity is said to "dance creation." The story pictures God as a great dancer, and the whole living world is pictured as the very dance of God. If the dancer were to stop dancing, the dance itself—the world—would cease to be. According to this story, we can hear music everywhere because all that exists is caught up in the single great cosmic dance, from the rhythmic swirl of galaxies to the vibration of tiny subatomic particles, from choruses of birds at sunrise to the gurgle of water cascading over the face of a mountain. God is dancing it all.

Both Don and Emily remember as children singing the hymn "For the Beauty of the Earth." Both of us were always intrigued by this stanza:

> For the joy of ear and eye, for the heart and mind's
> delight,
> for the mystic harmony linking sense to sound
> and sight,
> God of all, to you we raise, this our song of grateful
> praise.

What grabbed us here are the idea that "ear and eye" bring a joy that ultimately links us to God and the idea of "sense [and] sound and sight" linked together in some kind of "mystic harmony." These possibilities spoke to us deeply as musicians and as people who long for God. They spoke somehow to our intuition that music can take us out of ourselves and into the realm of the spirit. But how can this be?

We are intrigued by a musical image that Augustine of Hippo, a fifth-century theologian, used as he tried to express his deepest spirituality. "When I love you, what do I love?" he asks God. "Not the body's beauty, nor time's rhythm, nor light's brightness . . . nor song's sweet melodies, nor the fragrance of flowers, lotions and spices, nor manna and honey, nor the feel of flesh embracing flesh—none of these are what I love when I love my God." He believes that God is beyond what he can encounter by the eye, the ear, the skin, the tongue. And yet, and yet . . . he also believes that his senses bring him close to the understanding he seeks. "And yet, it's something like light, sound, smell, and touch that I love when I love my God—the light, voice, food, fragrance, embrace of my inner self, where a light shines for my soul. . . . *That's* what I love when I love my God!"

Sensible joy and delight in creaturely things are, for Augustine, strong clues for imagining what loving God might be. To say what loving God is like is to appeal to a whole series of senses. In his *Confessions,* Augustine refers to the beautiful melodies of the psalms he heard in Milan when he went to worship there. He wept with joy at the liberating "delights of the ear" that he experienced in singing psalms and hymns with his teacher, Ambrose, another great theologian of the ancient church, one remembered partly for his strong encouragement of music.

At the same time, Augustine was never fully comfortable with the delight he found in music. On occasion he grew fearful that his sensual engagement with melodies would distract him from the "pure" hearing of sacred Scripture. The Christian tradition inherited Augustine's ambivalence about sound and music, especially when music is joined to the texts of prayer. This ambivalence has also complicated the church's interpretation of other kinds of sensual engagement as well—and indeed of the body itself.

The two of us reject this ambivalence and embrace the joy of music. At the same time, we also recognize a tension between what we can create as musicians and our sense of the overwhelming character of the divine. Yet this tension can be a fruitful one, as it urges us on to become more and more open and attentive as musicians and listeners. When Don plays certain pieces of Bach on the organ in this spirit, he can visualize great heights and spaces. When Emily listens to certain Brazilian songs, even though she doesn't know Portuguese, she sees images and landscapes she has never visited. Both of us are aware, however, that receiving these gifts, these visions, has required effort—it has grown out of discipline over time. In this sense the deepening of spirituality is not a matter of ideas in the brain but rather the result of a disciplined lived experience that requires attention and practice.

PRACTICING ATTENTION, EMBODYING RITUAL, REMEMBERING OUR LIVES

For several years in the late sixties and early seventies, our family lived in the inner city of New Haven, Connecticut. The four Saliers daughters, including Emily, were quite young. They learned a set of ritual songs from neighborhood children, almost all of whom were African American. The children would form a circle with jump ropes. Calling out to one another across the swinging ropes, they began to sing. One at a time the children would dance into the circle, hop a few steps, then dance away, all the while singing amid the whirling ropes: "Miss Mary Mack, Mack, Mack . . . all dressed in black, black, black . . . with silver buttons, buttons, buttons, all down her back, back, back." This song and play told a story and became, in a sense, a ritual. It was clear that the kids had to learn to accent the words just so if they were to get the rhythm right, but the movements were often improvised. Some of the jumpers were real virtuosos; the steps became quite complex, yet all the time the basic melody and rhythm were sung out by all. The rules were clear: don't miss the skips, know the words, perform this song, and dance in the right spirit.

The children learned the words, the song, and the dance all together. Performing led to an ever-deepening delight and a kind of community of joy. This image of those singing, dancing children remains for Don a wonderful metaphor for how worship can move people. Emily remembers the children's voices and faces so clearly. We might call this a natural language of praise, discovered within the fusion of ordered sound, physical effort, and a communal sense of play. The children were formed in a joyful multisensory doing of their ritual musical game. The sounds of the whirling rope, the sounds of feet on the earth, the squeals of delight combined with the music in performance formed in them a kind of body memory. And the sense of doing something together is forever in that image. This is a spontaneous community of musical practice.

The body remembers shared music and sound long after the mind may be dimmed. Those children had sound, pitch, and rhythm in their bodies. All of these things are in what human beings do in our working, our playing, and our solemn occasions of grieving or rejoicing. Whether around campfires, in fields of harvest, or in temples and churches, the communal act of singing and listening to music has formed and expressed deep human emotions. Such emotions are not simply passing feelings; they are part of having a sense of being in the world. If music is the language of the soul made audible, then human voices conjoined in community are primary instruments of the soul, and thus a medium for expressing what goes beyond the immediate, commonsense world. All such musical experiences help us see that hearing and sound encode more than what we hear.

We remember life experiences and human relationships in and through ordered sound. Could we say that the music encodes our associations and feelings and gives them back to us again? If a parent and child shared a certain song at bedtime years ago, hearing it again can bring back memories decades old. Think of your own memory of human voices and the vivid memory of places and times when particular music was sounded.

Nothing brings this home more vividly than some cases of Alzheimer's disease. Often the last way of helping someone who has Alzheimer's be present is to play or sing songs from their childhood. A family friend shared this story with us:

> My husband had been gradually going downhill with Alzheimer's. At first we didn't know what was happening, just that he kept forgetting things, but eventually he was diagnosed. The kids and I decided that he should stay at home as long as possible. But we rarely took him out, even to church. This was a relief, in a sense, because going out always made him confused, and all of us were embarrassed for him around old church friends he could no longer name.

Then one Sunday when our daughter and son were home from college we just decided to go to church together. By this time, my husband had almost stopped speaking, and he usually could not even recognize his own children. So we were nervous about this outing, and we made sure to sit in a pew toward the back of the church. My husband sat silently through much of the service. Then suddenly, when the congregation rose to sing after the offering, he too stood up, straight as could be, and joined in: "Praise God from whom all blessings flow . . ." He didn't miss a note! We were dumbfounded, and tears streamed down our faces. It was like a little miracle. For a glorious moment, he was alive to us and to something outside himself—all because this song and these words were imprinted so deep inside him.

This story reminds us of how deeply music reaches into life. It is as though music gifts us with a lasting sense of the way the world feels. The philosopher Suzanne K. Langer says that "the real power of music lies in the fact that it can be 'true' to the life of feeling in a way that language cannot." Hearing ordered sound holds up to our ears and to all our senses the pattern of how we actually experience the world. Singing with others in worship, as this man had done for decades, requires deep memory and focused attention. The act of singing praise, lament, thanksgiving, or prayer to God goes beyond the surface of the words and beyond the passing sound of the voices. Singing and hearing music that expresses human life before the divine confers a special dignity on the singers and the hearers. If the words and the musical forms are adequate to the mystery of being human—to suffering and joy—then the sound itself becomes a medium of formation and transformation. Music is not simply an ornament of something already understood in words. Rather, ordered sound mediates the world to our senses and animates—literally, ensouls—those who enter it deeply.

For all these reasons, both of us are convinced that music is basic to any spiritual perception of the world, opening up the world and the rhythms of our lives whether we are making music or listening to it. Be attentive, and you will know that all people are far more than mere consumers of music and song. Our world opens up to us in surprising ways when we open ourselves to music. A favorite hymn puts it this way: "When in our music God is glorified, and adoration leaves no room for pride, it is as though the whole creation cried, 'Alleluia!'" But we have also known the songs of gladness, the melodies of justice, and the dirges of lament far beyond the boundaries of the church. So welcome to the journey into a "sound" spirituality. Perhaps through attentiveness to the music that is too often taken for granted (both outside and inside us), we may receive something unexpected—the whole stretch of human life, heightened and deepened by the presence of ordered sound.

Chapter 3

MY LIFE FLOWS ON IN ENDLESS SONG

—

The Indigo Girls' song about Virginia Woolf, the English novelist who died in 1941, tells of how Woolf's words came to Emily as if they were carried by "telephone lines through time." As a young woman ponders her own life while reading the diary of a woman from a past generation, she hears "the voice at the other end . . . like a long-lost friend" and realizes that even when "the apathy of time laughs in my face . . . each life has its place." When Don hears this song, he says, "I'm brought back to the sense of how precious life is and how Emily's song makes Woolf's words into a strong affirmation of life, even in the face of mortality." Emily feels that many fans who hear this song share Don's appreciation of its affirmation of life. "I sense that this song helps them carry a sense of being affirmed out into their own lives."

From Virginia Woolf to now and from one period in a person's life to another period, music carries us through time, even when our years have been fractured by pain and loss and mortality. We keep going back to certain songs because they contain something that is "like a message in a bottle" just for us, as Emily's song says. With some songs we discover the message over and over again, across the years.

Don often composes and leads musical settings of the psalms, which people sing together in churches. For him a line that works "like a telephone line through time" is a phrase from Psalm 139: "Search me, O God, and know my heart." Don says, "I keep coming back to this phrase, which speaks to me in the midst of so many life situations. In spite of everything I now know about human frailty and the threat of death, I always experience the affirmation of life when I return to this psalm. When I sing it, I feel that I am known and affirmed." Don recently composed a new musical setting for this psalm that features two voices, which the two of us then sang together at a musical event. As we sang—the first time we had sung together in public—both of us felt our hearts opening to a mysterious sense of being known by God. We sensed that offering this song to others as father and daughter somehow touched those who were listening very deeply as well.

Why do so many people keep going back to certain songs again and again? For both of us, it is a matter of searching for moments of insight, for the secrets in the words and music that have moved us, or for a sense of the illumination they once provided, like patches of light across our pathways. In returning to a song, we hope to find that light again, and we hope that it will lead us again to a little clearing in a dense forest. Just as people repeat rituals, we want to return again and again to certain music. Yet we don't expect to hear exactly the same thing we heard before, because sometimes even familiar songs and hymns suddenly expand into new experiences. Both of us, at different stages of our lives, have suddenly heard a new song hidden within what we thought was familiar. It may take a long time and perhaps some additional experience to get to the point where we can hear something we thought we knew and discover new dimensions. "Oh, now I see, now I hear, now I understand why that song got to me so deeply!"

In this chapter we explore some of the most elemental ways in which music helps us make sense of our lives. Ordered sound plays a primary role in human experiences, especially those we call religious or spiritual. When music is woven into our lives, it can bring a special artfulness to the patterns and rhythms of a life as it takes shape over time. Like most of you, both of us have experienced ways in which music interprets us—telling us who we are and where we are in life but also giving us intimations of what we and our world may yet become. We believe that one of the most basic reasons for music's power in these ways is that music always commingles and resonates with the cycles of time, across our individual lives, and across the lives of the communities to which we belong. Doing this, it shapes and expresses emotions, spirituality, identity, and ways of living in the world.

Living in Time with Music

"My life flows on in endless song," declares a nineteenth-century American hymn.

> Through all the tumult and the strife,
> I hear that music ringing.
> It finds an echo in my soul.
> How can I keep from singing?

We are temporal beings who live from one moment to the next, from one event to another, from one stage of life to the next; and if we are attentive, we can hear the rhythms of life given back to us in and through music. We are each bearers of the music that has accumulated in our experience of time. Voices and sounds from our past inhabit us. Music from our ancestors, songlines that we've inherited, sometimes without even recognizing them, suddenly become part of our awareness. Our surrounding social and natural world becomes more vivid when this happens. Sometimes it is only through song and music that we come to understand where we are along life's way.

Even though the two of us belong to two distinct generations, neither of us can forget the first time each of us heard Beethoven's Ninth Symphony and found that the final chorus, "Ode to Joy," opened a quality and meaning of cosmic ecstasy we could never have anticipated. Similarly, neither of us can forget the first time we were part of a crowd holding hands with crossed arms singing "We Shall Overcome" and how that opened up strong hope for a different future for our country. As we move through life, music echoes our emotions, deepens them, and gives us new ways of perceiving the world. It can reveal things we could not otherwise know.

In the previous chapter, we explored one crucial source of music's power in us: our bodies, which are built for and attuned to music. Sound strikes the ear, vibrates the whole body, enters consciousness, and becomes the language of our experienced world. Here we delve into a second reason music works so powerfully in and on us: music moves through time, and so do we. Some music can create great stillness within us, to be sure, but like life itself, music never really stands still. Music itself takes time—it cannot sound in an instant but always has some stretch and duration—and opening ourselves to music requires some of our own time. Music summons us to be fully present in the moment and in a sequence of moments, with a presence shaped to the music itself. As the one art form that cannot exist apart from the time it takes, music is innately temporal.

Even though it is a truism that contemporary people have short attention spans, Emily is always impressed that so many music fans seem to love long sets and are willing to go so far out of their way to attend concerts. When you consider how busy people are these days, it seems like something of a miracle that anyone in our frenetic culture takes the time to really listen to music. Something within us needs what music can give over time. Perhaps the secret within this miracle is that precisely because life today is so hectic and fragmented, people need the kind of deep immersion in time that music demands of its listeners—minutes and hours, measured out in rhythms and entered only through deep listening. For human beings who live within time—as all of us clearly do—this kind of deep entering into the moment can be redemptive, allowing us to be in time in a different way from the usual stress and hurry.

Music also takes time in another sense: it helps us see how we have changed over time by offering fresh meaning when we experience it for the second or the third or the hundredth time across the years. Think of the first time you heard a certain song about love—perhaps you and someone else called it "our song." How different it sounds ten or twenty years later, especially if you have moved on from this early love. The same dynamic also works with other kinds of songs. Both of us were caught off guard at Christmas in 2003 when we sang "O Little Town of Bethlehem." We had sung this carol hundreds of times before, but this time the newspapers were filled with stories and pictures of hatred and bloodshed in Bethlehem. We found the familiar lines deeply sobering, in a way they had not been in earlier Christmas seasons: "Yet in thy dark streets shineth the everlasting light; the hopes and fears of all the years are met in thee tonight." As we thought of the hopes and fears of both the Israelis and the Palestinians, we experienced in a new and powerful way our own deep yearning for peace and light in that place.

Singing Through the
Years of Our Lives

The music that resounds in our bodies, woven into time across the changes of a lifetime, is not only delightful; it is also crucial to our waking, sleeping, growing, indeed, to our coming to life as human beings. Music can be lavished on the little ones or withheld or only heard in harshness. Watching the youngest members of our family, now toddlers, begin to respond to song is one of life's mysterious joys. We've listened as their mothers sing lullabies, and we all chant nursery rhymes and talk a singsongy baby talk to them. Whenever Don can, he sits down at the piano keyboard with them on his lap or on the bench. They pound the keys in rhythm but soon pick out pitches, now high, now low. Something in those little minds and bodies responds with delight. And so the explicit music begins and with it the possibilities of spirit. The CD of Mozart played in the children's nursery does make a difference.

As children grow older, the practice of family singing around the table, whether in thanksgiving for food or simply as a way of sharing a song the children learned at school or in church, can bring great joy. Linking the times of family singing to larger communities opens a way for children (and parents) to glimpse what it means to be a hospitable household that also has a place within the larger household of God. Emily recalls how singing Christmas carols around the piano in the family living room was a highlight of the season. These songs were deeply ours, but we always knew that they were not ours alone. They also belonged to the Christian community as a whole. So it was also a great joy to sing these same songs at church or with friends at a party or to sing them for others when we visited nursing homes. In college Emily's sister Elizabeth worked in a retirement center and took Christmas songs and other family songs with her, to the delight of many.

One of our fondest family memories is of singing together on trips. None of us can forget one long car trip in our old Plymouth station wagon. Each of the four sisters in turn would start a song, and we would all join in until it finally sounded forth in six-part harmony. It was beautiful. But then, as Carrie, Jennie, and Emily were singing a lilting three-part song, Elizabeth began singing a half-tone off. We almost got through the whole thing but finally broke into uproarious laughter—so much so that Don had to pull the car off the road! As time has passed, we have come to see that what seemed at the time a nice thing to do together has bound us more closely together as a family. All of us share those memories, which are only made sharper by the music that is woven into them.

In adolescence music is often the element in which young people seek and find new insights or identity. Each sister had her own favorite artists. All of us recall when Emily first began listening to Joni Mitchell, who had a very strong initial influence on her music. Looking back, Emily explains how this felt:

> Joni Mitchell's song writing and singing were out
> of the ordinary. When she put something musi-
> cal together—the long story lines with her oddly

lyrical voice—I realized that no other musician was doing that. Her uniqueness came at a time in my life when I needed to grow. Her style was pointed, poetic, and so well crafted. When she did a jazz album, the jazz buffs said, "This isn't jazz." But neither did she conform to the popular styles at the time. I listened to the free form and heard something unique. Her own vocal harmonies were stacked, but she kept the melody flowing. She used bizarre guitar tunings (at least to me) and created a whole new approach to sound. I was captivated; now I could hear something new.

For Emily this was a breakthrough, a hearing that allowed her to begin to develop her own music in a deeper way.

Don had a comparable experience during college in his first encounters with the twentieth-century English composer Benjamin Britten. After his first encounters with Britten's opera *Peter Grimes,* his choral piece "Rejoice in the Lamb," and the *War Requiem,* Don says,

I wanted to listen over and over to Britten, because his music was changing what I could hear. He revealed things about putting sacred and secular texts together that opened a new world to me. Only recently, much later in life, have I returned to the *War Requiem* to meditate on the relationships between beauty and terror. In this great piece for orchestra, soloists, and chorus, Britten interweaves the terrifying poems Wilfred Owen wrote in the trenches during the First World War with the ancient text of the Christian

Mass—the prayers of praise, repentance, entreaty, and thanksgiving still offered by Catholics and some other Christians when they gather for worship and communion. I found myself beginning to grasp the depths of unresolved raw sorrow of Vietnam's aftermath in a new way. And recently, in hearing a performance of that same requiem, the destruction and suffering of current wars in Africa and in the Middle East crowded into the terrible tensions of Britten's music. At one point we hear the innocence of children singing prayers for the dead interwoven with the relentless slaying of human beings, "half the seed of Europe, one by one."

Each period of life brings new rhythms, new responses to music—perhaps never more than when those first stirrings of love for another person emerge and then develop through dating, courtship, covenant, marriage. Most couples can pinpoint a song that goes with the first time they met or their first date or first kiss or the night of a proposal. We lean forward eagerly to hear the stories behind these songs and to find how they connect with our own, even when they appear in the movies. "Play it again, Sam," says Humphrey Bogart's character in the film *Casablanca,* and the piano player launches into "As Time Goes By." As we say, "That's a classic!" From that scene and that song, we recall the rest of the story and get misty-eyed over love that was lost even though it is still cherished in the heart.

As we move from adolescence to adulthood, more and more memories are associated with particular songs.

Some—like "Happy Birthday"—recur like rituals. Birthdays in our family always combined the ritual cake and song with music and revelry. On Don and Jane's fortieth wedding anniversary, Emily and her sisters arranged a surprise party that included many of their parents' friends and colleagues. The song that time was "Happy Anniversary to You," sung with gusto as Don and Jane's blindfolds were removed. And then came the dancing—with a band that played the great danceable standards that the anniversary couple had grown up with, including tunes Don had played with his jazz group in college.

In our family it was not only personal anniversaries that called forth music and song. We also lived by the rhythm of seasons and holy days within our religious tradition. Each new year, for Christians, begins with the four Sundays of Advent, when we traditionally sing "O Come, O Come Emmanuel." Christmas follows, with its carols, which we sing through the twelve days of Christmas. The feast of the Epiphany in early January also has its own songs and hymns, leading into a season that continues all the way to Ash Wednesday, the beginning of the forty days of Lent. So we all knew "Lord, Who Throughout These Forty Days" and other hymns of this season as well, which ultimately leads to Holy Week and then to Easter. The sisters remember Palm Sunday by a classic hymn, "All Glory Laud and Honor," sung while processing with palm leaves, and Holy Week by its spirituals, including the mournful "Were You There When They Crucified My Lord?" After this sad and quiet music, the alleluias of the Easter hymns burst forth with joy. All these changing hymns and anthems and many others shaped the way we heard and experienced this passage through time. The great feasts and seasons echoing ancient biblical memory together with our community made remembering a musical matter.

Our lives do flow on in endless song, as we are carried from one moment to the next. Music accompanies us, opening up the poignancy of aging, of limits, of the passage of time. Don remembers playing an arrangement of the German-American composer Kurt Weill's great tune, "September Song," with his college jazz quintet. "O it's a long, long while, from May to December, but the days grow short, when you reach September." Playing the song as a young man in his twenties, he enjoyed improvising on a poignant love song. But now in his sixties, Don knows that the song interprets him and where he is in life very differently. It's like the experience you might have with a song heard and sung in childhood, such as "This little light of mine, I'm gonna let it shine." You hear it so differently later in life when you realize how small your light is and how dark the world can be.

Emily's song "Prince of Darkness" plays on a contrast, "my place is of the light, and this place is of the dark." Emily recalls that "Prince of Darkness" was written at a time in her life "when I was confronted by and trying to make sense of many forces in the world that brought destruction: the possibility of nuclear annihilation, addictions, and human cruelty. While some of the lines seem juvenile and overwrought now, I was wrestling with how to deal with life's dark sides and at the same time to reaffirm my commitment to move with the 'light.' This struggle goes on, but my life experiences point to deeper complexities and complicities in ways I couldn't see then." For both of us that song comes back years later to mean more than when she first wrote it, especially within the darkness of our present time of fear and terror.

In the end, music carries many of us right into old age. Don recalls interviewing a group of Methodist women in their eighties and nineties about what hymns and songs they loved and why. They responded with selections from the all-time church hit parade of golden oldies: "Blessed Assurance," "How Great Thou Art," "I Come to the Garden Alone," and of course, "Amazing Grace." These they had sung, some of them, for eighty years or more. When they began to say why they loved them, they spoke of hearing their grandmother's voice; of feeling the vibrations in their mothers' breast as they leaned against her in church; of the squeak of the parlor organ when the family would gather to sing; or of church suppers, funerals, or "dinner on the grounds" in their Southern traditions. They were speaking of the body memory of these songs and hymns. Something about their whole lives were encoded in the singing. Such is the power of music to carry us through life's passages.

MUSIC, THE TEMPORAL ART

One of Emily's songs, "History of Us," brought home for Don the power of music to deepen the experience of life

My Life Flows On in Endless Song

over time. Emily composed the song on our family trip to Europe, in honor of the sisters' graduations from high school and college. But when she first performed it in concert and her parents heard it for the first time, they didn't know that she had written it during that trip.

At first, Don thought it was a standard love song. "I went all the way to Paris to forget your face . . . all across the continent to relieve this restless love," it begins. The singer notices the statues of those whose lives ended long ago, the ruins created by wars, the faces in museum paintings, a sleeping village. Each scene tells of a time and place where human beings have loved and suffered. But in the midst of this, the singer also hears the call of "the living God" and understands the importance of her own "life here on earth" and of those dear to her, "the flock" she must keep. Each verse ends with a refrain that acknowledges pain and mortality while also singing strongly and hopefully of love:

> So we must love while these moments are still called today
> Take part in the pain of this passion play
> Stretching our youth as we must, until we are ashes to dust
> Until time makes history of us

Hearing this song for the first time at a benefit concert, Don was deeply moved as a father and as a listener. He remembers, "Why were these tears forming in my eyes? The song was indeed about love, but love under the aspect of time and mortality. As I remembered that family trip, I felt as if I had suddenly come across a photo album with pictures of another time and place. Now that past was made real and present again, in a living performance in song."

Emily recalls the trip vividly.

> We left for Europe the day I graduated from Emory. Surely I was in the throes of some romance. Initially, this song was a catharsis, a purging of emotions when love is stormy. But then I was awestruck by all the things we were witnessing: the dusty, ancient cathedrals, the packed Paris museums, the overwhelming majesty of the Alps. I began to collect images of the human search for immortality through art and ardor. I realized that our days are numbered and that today is really what we have. So, like good shepherds, we ought to tend the flocks we are given. A kind of great passion play of humanity stretched out before me, and there was no other way to think of my personal call except in terms of what's universal. Human striving continues, though finally we all turn to dust. The language of divine call seemed the deepest way to express a need for compassion in the face of our mortality. I simply tried in the song to come to terms with these things.

Some music first awakens us to the heartache of being alive, of passing through time. We gradually come to know our longings and yearnings through the music. This often connects different types of music we first think are totally unlike each other. In discussing how opera is so full of the drama of love and death and unfulfilled desire, a friend of ours who loves country music observed that the elevated music of opera and the down-home music of some country musicians are both about the aching heart.

Of course, there are vast differences between the operatic composer Giacomo Puccini and Johnny Cash; but if we listen, we can hear the longing and the heart-music of passing through time.

Music is the temporal art par excellence. Unlike painting or sculpture or architecture, music is by its very nature ephemeral. It sounds within a *now* that vanishes. Our present moments are fleeting. Yet music mysteriously connects the time past with the *now* and with what is to come. It invites us to appreciate the *now* that is past right in the midst of the *now* we inhabit in the present. And it opens our hearts to ache for the fulfillment to come. No wonder that music sounds the first and last notes of life and permeates human passages. The very flow of life is given back to us in music that can touch that deeply in our bodies and souls. What we must do, of course, is learn how to listen and how to hear.

In the making of both so-called secular and so-called sacred music, there are times when the future breaks in:

My life flows on in endless song;
above earth's lamentation
I catch the sweet, though far-off hymn
that hails a new creation.

Chapter 4

DO YOU HEAR
WHAT I HEAR?

———

D ad! Listen to this!" Like many who have raised
teenagers, Don has had the experience of having
his daughters ask him to appreciate recordings
that were not exactly to his initial taste or interest. "OK,
sure," he remembers responding as he tried to hide his
reluctance. Emily remembers that she and her sisters
sometimes felt the same way about the classical pieces he
made them endure. But over the years, we have come to
treasure each other's invitations to listen. "Do you hear
that passage?" "Listen to how this is phrased." "Isn't that
an amazing voice?" We have learned so much from one
another as a result. Don now listens much more attentively to Patti Smith or to hip-hop fusion because of what
Emily has helped him to hear. At the same time, Emily
says, "Thanks for helping me hear Bach and Mahler in a
new way and also some contemporary church composers
like Christopher Willcock and Richard Proulx." Occa-
sionally, we have also been blessed with the opportunity to
discover a new sound together, as when we first listened

to a recording of Bulgarian women's voices. "They sound just like reed instruments!" we both exclaimed.

This kind of sharing goes on all the time between the generations, between friends, between peers. Getting someone else to listen to the music you love, the music that moves you, is a unique pleasure—just as telling your friends, "Try it, you'll like it" about an unfamiliar ethnic food you really enjoy is also a pleasure. But when people share music, they exchange more than taste. When a friend really listens to the unfamiliar music you have shared, when the friend really hears it, you realize that you have allowed your friend a glimpse into your soul. Music shared deeply makes a soul connection.

Listening, really listening, is a practice that is difficult and sometimes even dangerous. Deep attentive listening has the power to draw us into the mystery called silence. Often in listening, we encounter other people and our own lives in new ways.

Offering Attention in a World of Sound

Our ancestors were far more alert to the sounds in their natural surroundings than we are. In some ways their lives depended on attentiveness to sound, which could provide clues to such life-threatening realities as small changes in the weather or the presence of a predator. In his memorable book *The Spell of the Sensuous,* ecologist and philosopher David Abram explores how those living in a sheerly oral culture, without written texts, became attuned to the "voices" of nature, so closely attuned that the very sounds of their own speech—its "rhythms, tones, and inflections"—reflected "the contour and scale of the local landscape . . . the visual rhythms of the local topography." Abram reminds us that the human voice and ear have been attentive "to the various nonhuman calls and cries that animate the local terrain" from time immemorial.

Don's longtime friend and colleague Alice Parker, an exceptional and influential composer, arranger, and enabler of communal singing, is also persuaded of the overwhelming importance of listening in shaping our ability to engage with the world and with one another. When she works with a choir, Parker often begins with a time of deep listening to the tones and rhythms of words, helping those who sing with her to develop a rich sensitivity to oral language—to how words sound when spoken and sung. Composers and performers may have to learn to listen with a depth and finesse not necessary for most people, to be sure, but Parker is convinced that with disciplined practice everyone can learn to listen far more acutely than they usually do. After all, she notes, all of us first learned to speak and to sing by listening to others and then imitating them. We began by rote; only later did our skill and appreciation for the range of ordered sound grow. So let's listen and imitate and grow some more, she urges.

As one who treasures what she calls "the congregational voice," Alice Parker especially seeks to awaken a close and mutual listening and responsiveness among those who sing together in worship. "It can and should be beautiful, meaningful, musical, full of the Spirit, responsive to both text and tune, and magnetic in drawing together all who hear," she writes in her aptly titled book *Melodious Accord*. Alice doesn't just write about this; the magnetism happens when she works with a group of ordinary voices.

Distracted as we are in our present age, we rarely take the time to listen closely to the human voices that surround us. Sometimes it seems that the whole culture is just too busy to listen. For example, we rarely encounter the beauty of poetry read aloud—a beauty that inches close to music. Both of us have memories of the voices of our grade school teachers (and even of some specific phrases) as they read aloud in class—memories that remain a great delight. Today's public poetry, on the other hand, tends to be advertising jingles. What happens to our human capacity to hear when so much of the poetry, the recorded speech, and the singing we hear is trying to sell us something? In such a cultural context, the opportunity to open our ears and listen to live music, and sometimes also to join in with our own voices, is incredibly precious, whether it happens in schools or in places of worship.

LISTENING WITH OUR WHOLE SELVES

Don is sometimes overwhelmed by the energy of the large crowds who respond to Emily and Amy at live concerts. In these situations it becomes obvious that listening involves a lot more than the ears: listening involves the whole self, body and all. The same fact becomes clear when you see a small child who starts moving when she hears a favorite song: she twists her body, raises her hands, and looks to you as if asking for a dance. When we really listen, music gets to us with a depth that can take us by surprise.

When you try to describe a song or piece of music that has caught your attention, it's natural to begin by saying how it makes you feel. You may find yourself realizing that a certain song or musical piece puts you in a particular mood—romantic or sad or joyful or even some strange poignant mix of all three. Some music is simply flat-out erotic and physical because of the beat, of course, but other music is more subtle. It makes us search for the right words to describe the mood it stirs up in us. Emily often has someone tell her that her song "The Power of Two" has given them hope or that "Closer to Fine" lifts their spirits. She in turn has found that many of Joni Mitchell's songs give her the gift of true feeling in a way few other songs can do.

Listening can tap into the imagination in other ways as well, beyond mood and emotion. If you listen to Maurice Ravel's piece "Bolero," you may begin to experience how relentless, yet how interesting, the many and varied colors and textures in this music are, swirling around as the same melody is repeated over and over again. Or you may find that a certain organ prelude and fugue by Bach gives you the sense of great space and architecture, as if someone were building a great cathedral in sound. The contemporary Polish composer Henryck Górecki creates in many listeners a sense of the vast inner spaces of contemplation. The voices of the women who are the Anonymous Four, chanting a medieval Mass, can make you wish you knew Latin so that you could understand and grasp the beauty of "An English Ladymass" even more deeply.

One morning not long ago, while driving to the cabin where we did some of our writing, the two of us listened to a CD of medieval Icelandic songs. *Epitaph* contains ancient chants as well as songs with folk origins. If you've ever heard someone speak Icelandic, you know that its sounds are remote from English; and the accompaniment by medieval instruments made this music seem even more distant from our own experience. But together we fell into silent, intense listening and entered a completely different world than the one we were driving through. We were absolutely mesmerized and did not speak for quite a while after the music ended. Then we shared our feelings about having entered an alien landscape that riveted our imaginations through peculiar musical lines shaped by bare harmonics and surprising combinations of sound. And we talked about the uncanny beauty of a language we did not understand—all while driving back into a familiar cove in the North Georgia mountains that would never quite be the same because of that hearing.

Emily had not known the Icelandic recording before. But neither had Don listened to Joni Mitchell before Emily, then sixteen, brought home a record she had just discovered. She would say, "Do you hear that—the way the voice and the guitar and the gentle shift in percussion work?" Though that was years ago, Don says, "I have always appreciated that introduction. I began to hear something I hadn't heard before, a style that I continue to find interesting and rich." Similarly, Emily has heard many new things in Don's organ playing, which often features improvisation. "I heard something in what you played on the organ at the end of worship last Sunday—part of that improvisation," she told him recently. "Did you intend to evoke irony in that old hymn tune?" Don confessed that he did not, but he also thanked her for listening so closely and thus alerting him to this nuance in his playing. At other times his listening to the blend of voices and instruments in one of her live performances has helped her to hear her own music more fully as well.

SOUNDING THE ELEMENTS OF MUSIC

Both of us work with sounds. But how do sounds, rightly disciplined and ordered, become music that affects us so deeply in feeling and memory? What makes sound become music? And how do many sounds work together to make rich and memorable music?

Emily has spent a lot of time in recording studios.

> When we go into the studio to make a record, we have to consider many elements in the construction of the music. Each element has to have its own space in relation to all the other elements. Typically, we don't want a complex drum or instrumental part to overwhelm or compete with a particular melody line. Sometimes an intricate

keyboard passage part is lost in the rhythmic element, or it doesn't suit the lyrics of a particular phrase. In the mixing process, we are careful not to have competing elements in the same sound spectrum. Parts can effectively cross each other out when the sound space is too crowded. So we strive for a well-constructed pattern and use of all the elements. Each element can stand out on its own at times, but the final musical event must respect how the parts work together to achieve the beauty, the clarity, and the communicative power of the whole piece. This is, for me, a metaphor for humanity. Each voice has its place, but only in sounding together in a focused way can you realize what each has to contribute.

Rhythm is a core element in music just as it is a core element in life. Perhaps the first thing we hear in the womb is the sound of our mother's heartbeat, the flow of blood through the veins and arteries, and then later the sounds from outside the womb. All of these keep time as we await our entry into the world. Don recalls playing a recording of Stravinsky's *Rite of Spring* for a pregnant friend, turning up the sound at a certain point. The child in her womb leapt vigorously, knocking her cup of tea right off her stomach! Who knows what little Sarah-in-the-womb thought? (Incidentally, she grew up to be a dancer.) Perhaps the pull to move to the beat of a drum and the instinct to gravitate toward its rhythmic sound hark back to our very elemental roots, the first song of life.

Emily remembers a time when a strongly beaten rhythm united a group on a serious mission. "On a rickety boat going from Vieques back to the mainland of

Puerto Rico, a young man tapped a beat out on the metal railing. And this beat brought on a song. My friend Lourdes immediately began singing a song to the rhythm—a song to protest the U.S. Navy's bombing exercises on their tiny island. Before we reached land, the whole boatload of people was singing to the rhythm of the tapping." Another time, Emily was standing near the edge of the stage during a benefit concert for indigenous environmental groups while a local drum group was playing. A woman next to her leaned in to say, "That drum is the heart of my people."

The last sixty years have been rich with permutations of rhythm—the backbeat of rock and roll, the syncopation of hip-hop, the intricate beats of progressive jazz. Drum rhythms brought from Africa forever changed the face of American music of all types.

As basic and essential as rhythm is, when we listen we are usually more attentive to melody. Melody is the chief element of song and the most memorable, especially when words are woven into the melodic line. It is the great gift of folk music traditions but also the glory of classical music and the sine qua non of popular music. Just overhearing a fragment of a treasured melody may flood the attentive listener with emotion, as the melody evokes love, pain, beauty, or ugliness. Franz Schubert's song cycles are masterpieces of melody, expressing the bittersweet sound of life. Operagoers love Puccini, Verdi, Mahler, or Mozart for their melody—but especially melody linked to deep feeling.

Another important element of music, harmony, may be its least acclaimed but most valuable part. When young children move from learning to sing a little melody to singing in parts, a whole new world opens. Making a round of even the simplest song ("Row, row, row your boat" or "White coral bells upon a slender stalk") introduces two or more lines and notes at once, greatly increasing the song's beauty and interest. Piano lessons that begin with single lines progress to lines that use both hands simultaneously, sounding several notes at once. Gradually, the harmonies grow more complex, as chord changes carry the music forward and prepare us to hear larger chords and more complex keys. Don recalls hearing an orchestra for the first time and being astounded by the sound of all those instruments playing different parts at once: "The world seemed to expand through my ears. And now I sit by my grandson at his first symphony concert and grin as he exclaims 'Wow!' at the *William Tell Overture*."

And then there is tempo: music played slowly, then fast, then faster still. Is it really possible to play Chopin's "Minute Waltz" in a minute? Don accomplished this feat but only after years of practicing scales religiously, especially in the key of D-flat. As music becomes more complex, it gathers force from other elements as well. Sounds, musicians say, have color. And rhythms and melodies sometimes give way to counterpoint. Johann Sebastian Bach, the great eighteenth-century composer, was the great genius of counterpoint, which relies on simultaneous multiple melodic lines. And counterpoint also marks the duet style of much of the Indigo Girls' music.

It takes real study to learn to analyze music into its elements, listening for them and seeing how they work together. Composers must do so, and performers also have to listen in this way. With musician friends we sit and say, "Oh, listen to that line, that harmony!" This is how musicians talk, but so do nonmusicians who want to share their passion for what they are hearing. All who listen may come to hear more and more deeply with practice over time.

As a teacher of music, Don admits that sometimes he has to listen very analytically; but he also knows that the real joy comes when finally it is time to experience the music again as a whole sound. Emily comments,

> In the recording studio, Amy and I spend a lot of time analyzing the different elements that go together in a particular song: the bass line, the keyboard part, the drums, acoustic guitar parts, the vocal lines, pitch levels, the tempo. We work with these things. And with digital technology, we now are capable of moving things around. Repairing mistakes now involves a much more self-conscious construction of the music than when we began nearly twenty years ago. Attentiveness to small individual elements is crucial. After months of making a record, I can't listen without picking out all the different elements. Listening so analytically is partly an uncomfortable experience. It robs me for a while of hearing the whole of it. I anxiously wait for this to pass. And eventually it does.

There is pleasure in taking music apart, in appreciating all the elements, but there is also a different and very great pleasure in experiencing the music whole. When Emily says that she wants "to feel the way music makes me feel," Don agrees but says he can't help admiring the sheer pattern and formal structures of sound in the music because he wants "to understand the forms." Again we find ourselves paying attention to different features but always learning from one another.

HEARING THE SILENCES

Even though it is not obvious at first, silence is crucial to music. Listening and coming to hear what music offers is in part a matter of learning to appreciate silence. What is not sounded is as important as what is. A major part of any composer's craft is listening for the yet unheard note, straining to hear the voice that is yet to sound through the silence—the note, the voice that will address the mounting expectation.

The spaces between musical notes and phrases are as important as the notes themselves. In this sense music is similar to conversation. If you think about it, the pauses we make between words are not only for emphasis or dramatic effect. Rather, the unsounded spaces between words and phrases help us to understand one another. If all our words ran together with no rhythm and without pauses, our communication would not only lack subtlety, it would be incomprehensible. Remember when you have tried and failed to understand someone who was talking in great haste. "Slow down, I can't understand you," you may finally have cried. Although we don't ordinarily notice all the little silences that sprinkle our speech, we would surely notice their absence. Well-placed silences allow us to take in what the speaker is saying.

Silence also frames our experience of the natural world. In order to hear a bird's distinctive song, we must learn to be still and listen. Recently in Vermont, as Don walked a forest path at twilight, an absolutely pure four-note bird call pierced the stillness. Then came silence. "I hoped that the bird would continue the song, so I stopped," Don recalls. "Then the silence of the woods was broken by that same call once again. The little concert went on for some time. The silences and the song are now part of my memory of that path and that place." This encounter reminded Don of R. S. Thomas's poem, "Evening," which speaks of the "interval of our wounding silence turned golden."

It should be no surprise, given its importance, that silence can both wound and turn golden. Music in which silence is skillfully arrayed alongside vivid sound can have special power to wound us with beauty while also evoking great yearning. Consider the famous opening of Beethoven's Fifth Symphony. Those powerful first four notes have great impact precisely because they are framed by dramatic silences. Many listeners—including the two of us—respond almost viscerally, tensing up to await what comes next. However, if a listener doesn't pay attention and really *hear* those opening measures, he or she may miss the power of the whole first movement, which Beethoven built on the foundation of those four notes.

All live music begins in silence, as musicians and listeners ready themselves for the emergence of ordered sound. Different kinds or pieces of music break the silence in different ways—explosively for Beethoven in the Fifth, or gently, with fingers strumming six strings, for a folksinger doing a ballad. And some music not only breaks silence but also summons forth silence as a response; you sit there after listening and just want to be still. In any case, silence is not simply a meaningless absence of sound; it frames and shapes sound in ways that make each piece of music what it is. Becoming aware of how crucial silence is can help you to appreciate both the sounds and the space between the sounds more fully. Coming to this awareness is worth some effort, even if it means turning off the background music that permeates so many places today.

On one of their tours, Amy and Emily chose to end their concert—a nearly two-hour set of rocking, wide-ranging music, with plenty of amplified volume—with a quiet, a cappella version of "Finlandia": "This is my song, O God of all the nations, a song of peace for lands afar and mine." Don, who heard the concert in Atlanta, was deeply moved as the dancing, stage-pressing crowd quieted down to a whisper. The quiet singing, ringing in close harmony through the stillness, caught them, and they began to listen with deep attention to the words of this urgent song of peace. Perhaps the fans were still because of the pull that human voices alone exerted after a long set that included many instruments, or perhaps the stillness fell because the song came at the end of a long and energizing evening. In any case, the audience was clearly ready to take a breath. Don believes that the reasons for the fans' quiet appreciation were the music and the performers—the simplicity, the close harmony, the directness of the words and musical communication, the seemingly artless artistry. That enthusiastic, boisterous crowd grew still, and all the listeners' faces and bodies concentrated in a moment of sheer meditative focus.

A moment like this draws us very close to meditation and perhaps even to prayer. This is not the quiet of boredom but the silence of intensity, a quality common to music and to contemplative prayer alike.

Lingering in silence is a remarkable experience— and one that frazzled people desperately need. This need accounts in part, we believe, for the love many people are developing for the quiet, meditative music of Taizé, an ecumenical community in France that is teaching Christians around the world an ancient yet new way to worship. *"Ubi caritas et amor, Deus ibi est"* ("Where there is charity and love, there is God," with the text in Latin to enable those from many language groups to join as equals)—a community can softly sing these words, again and again, for an hour or more, joined perhaps by flutes or quiet vocal solos. Based on musical forms and harmonies used by Christians in previous centuries, this music brings rich prayer texts together with singable melodies. Those who sing Taizé music over and over often develop an increasing appreciation, as familiarity draws them to a place of deep rest.

Don recently attended a Taizé service near San Francisco that was overflowing with young people. For nearly two hours, those gathered sang meditative music, pausing for long silences between the chants. At the high point of the service, people took turns coming forward to a place of prayer, where they knelt in circles around a central icon surrounded by lighted candles. The whole experience was one of great stillness and centering. Afterward Don asked two young women why they were there. "This is the one place we can find ourselves quieting down in a crazy world," both replied. "It's here that God catches up with us; here we can listen for God."

A recent hymn that joins the poetry of Jaroslav Vajda and the music of Carl Schalk incorporates silence into the text and structure of the music. The hymn involves a community that is receiving Holy Communion (also called participating in Eucharist or the Lord's Supper) in singing a description of what faith tells them is happening in their midst. It is at once both dramatically active and deeply, contemplatively quiet. As the music unfolds, the palpable sense of the silent mystery of the holy meal is realized.

> Now the silence
> Now the peace
> Now the empty hands uplifted
> Now the kneeling
> Now the plea
> Now the Father's arms in welcome

Then, as the melody raises in pitch and intensity, the assembly sings

> Now the hearing
> Now the power
> Now the vessel brimmed for pouring . . .
> Now the wedding
> Now the songs
> Now the heart forgiven leaping

Then, at the height of the song, a strongly repetitive musical line:

> Now the Spirit's visitation
> Now the Son's epiphany
> Now the Father's blessing

Then, finally, gently, softer and softer,

> Now
> Now
> Now

The practice of attentive listening, which requires us to become still so that we can hear the silence as well as the sound, is a great treasure in the sonic, often chaotic, world we inhabit. Although Emily and Don sometimes disagree over which music is worth listening to, we agree that attentive listening is an art that can heal and reveal.

LISTENING FOR (AND WITH) THE SOUL

Throughout our lives both of us have experienced the sense that music expresses and shapes our emotions. Strong emotional connection with music is not something that usually emerges when we just happen to be around some background music, however. The depth and authenticity of the feelings that music summons up are often related to the carefulness with which we listen. The song or hymn or symphony is the tapestry of feeling, but it becomes ours only when we bring something of ourselves to the listening. In careful listening, as the music theorist Thomas Clifton writes, we are asked to "match [the music's] feeling, to rise to the occasion." When this happens, we "recognize" the music, and we sometimes feel as if the music recognizes us as well.

Depth and mystery are characteristic of human beings and also characteristic of many musical pieces. "All persons—and some works of art—have souls that are complex, multilayered, and partly hidden," writes the British philosopher Mary Mothersill. "They are not to be taken in at a glance, and long study leaves room for fresh discoveries." In her discerning but challenging book *Beauty Restored,* Mothersill argues that we human beings have a fundamental need for beauty and celebrates our capacity to give our attention to beauty: "Some things like a pebble, or a clear and cloudless sky, have simple souls," she notes; these are pleasing but do not invite prolonged attention. Some other things are attractive at first but lack substance. But still others have a complexity and substance that can keep us enthralled for a lifetime. These things she calls "deep souls," inexhaustibly rich—such as music we can keep listening to as our own life experience grows.

Music, with all its great variety, is like this. Some music lacks soul. Some songs and pieces have what Mothersill calls "simple souls," and some music is inexhaustibly "deep souled." The latter requires us to listen again and again and always allows new discoveries. Each new performance, and each new sharing among listeners, has the potential for sounding new dimensions and revealing new depths of silence, feeling, and insight.

The surprise here is that the question of soul is not a matter of classical versus popular or folk music. Nor is it a matter of secular versus sacred music. Some years back a certain African American style came to be called "soul music," but a Mahler symphony or Bach's *Goldberg Variations* also displays something that can only be called soul. Whether in popular or in classical music, however, encountering the soul of a piece of music cannot be taken for granted; rather, this encounter requires us to listen attentively to discover what is actually sounded in the music. Only those who develop a soul for hearing can hear the soul of music.

Developing a soul for hearing takes time; it cannot be rushed. This is not necessarily because you have to be able to deal with a certain musical complexity. Rather, it is partly because you will be able to hear more as you become more complex as a person. Certain songs won't disclose themselves fully to someone who isn't ready; in fact, some seem to be just waiting for you to experience life. For both of us, "Amazing Grace" is like that. The tune is not exceptional, but the way it is joined to the words touches us powerfully. The longer we have lived, the more we have been able to appreciate the role of grace in life and how amazing it is. This song speaks to us even though we don't take the words about being a "wretch" literally or think that getting saved has to happen in a specific moment. What we relate to is the powerful experience of coming to "see" when once you were "blind" to some crucial reality. This kind of transformation comes from beyond the normal human run of events and even our best human capacities. Singing or listening to this song, in fact, it is possible to remember not only a specific instance of grace but also to see that all good and all beauty come by grace.

"How often making music we have found a new dimension in the world of sound," writes the British hymn writer Fred Pratt Green in one of his many marvelous hymns—this one a hymn of thanks to God for music. Making music, the hymn continues, leads us somewhere; it does something to us. It leads us, writes Green, to "a more profound 'Alleluia.'" Alleluia—the summation of God's praise, a glorious *yes* to life itself.

This new dimension in the world of sound—drawing us in, leading us somewhere, doing things to us— keeps us making and listening to music. And how often, as Pratt Green notes, it leads us to praise. Not always, to be sure, but oh, how often! In Jewish and Christian traditions, the resulting alleluia is the sound of praise offered to the Creator of everything that is. We write these pages convinced that echoes of such an alleluia can be found whenever and wherever human beings gather to sing together about their hope, courage, gratitude, and joy.

Chapter 5

BECOMING WHO WE ARE THROUGH MUSIC

——

When the Indigo Girls first performed Amy Ray's song "Become You" live, Don was immediately captivated by its strong musical lines. Only a little later did he begin to perceive the depth of the words. In this song a white woman who was born and raised in the South reflects on the mixed social legacy she has inherited. And a powerful truth comes over her: it takes a long time to become who we are as persons and as communities, for good and for ill.

Living with music over the course of many years is something like living in a certain part of the country: it plays a strong role in how you become you. Both of us are convinced that music plays a much bigger role in your becoming who you are than many people realize. For the two of us—and for many others—music has been crucial to finding personal identity and discovering the communities to which we belong. It has been for us and can be for others a strong and positive force in discovering who we are and yet may become.

WHAT IS IT ABOUT THAT MUSIC?

Emily recalls driving to a rehearsal one morning many years ago and hearing an orchestral piece on the radio. "It held me captive," she remembers. "I had to pull over to hear the rest of it. There was a storm brewing outside, and one of the movements was itself like a movement of dark clouds swelling in intensity with suspension and resolution. Something in the music was a wordless interpretation of the mystery of the weather." And the music? It was the twentieth-century English composer Edward Elgar's piece *Enigma Variations*—the fourteenth variation, to be exact. Emily had never heard this piece before. As she sat there in her car, she knew that this music was powerful in this moment because it was so much like the storm. "The piece became life and at the same time made life larger than life or as infinitely wide as I could have experienced it." But looking back, she and Don began to wonder if a second reason this music was so riveting was because it stirred up deep memories of the orchestral music that permeated her childhood. Was it possible that she could really hear this music and enter deeply into its moods because it resonated with childhood memories of concerts by live symphony orchestras or with recorded music that played in the family home?

The music that sounded through the house or in the streets where you grew up stays in your mind and body for the rest of your life, even when you aren't conscious of it. This is part of how each person comes to belong to a culture. Our ears pick up a certain vocal style or a particular pattern of rhythm; and we find ourselves listening intently, resonating to the memory of a grandmother's hymns or a father's violin. You know in your bones that a particular set of sounds is yours: you belong to it, and it belongs to you. Sometimes we say, "I just can't get that song out of my head."

Although cultural identity is part of what makes us sit up and listen, however, it is not the only reason we do so. The first time Emily heard the Brazilian music of D'Javan or the Arabic singing of Natacha Atlas, she felt "an immediate soul connection to the music that was inexplicable to me." Both of us have had the startling experience of having completely unfamiliar music suddenly opening up unexpected parts of our selves. This has happened to us with a Native American drumbeat, on the first hearing of Miles Davis's "cool" trumpet, or just recently at the playing of a didgeridoo by an Australian Aboriginal musician. A certain vocal sound, a particular pattern of rhythm, gets through in a powerful way, and we find ourselves paying attention, listening hard.

What we listen to will shape how and what we sing. A child growing up in Seoul, Korea, sings differently than a child growing up in the mountains of Peru or in backcountry Nigeria, singing in the musical mother tongue. We all have home-culture music, but that is not all we have. We also have the ability to hear new things.

Learning to play an instrument or to sing, we deliberately cross over into other people's music. Encountering unfamiliar music at a concert, on our travels, or—this may surprise you—at church, we listen to others in new ways.

The same dynamic of crossing over exists between generations. Young people seem instinctively to resist their elders' music, as if to say, "Whatever *they* found meaningful in this music, we do not!" This fact is obvious in American culture, especially since the advent of rock 'n' roll. This is not to say that all resistance and rebellion are a conscious project; sometimes it is the culture itself that changes. Bob Dylan sang in the 1960s "The Times, They Are A-Changin'"—a song that no longer speaks in quite the same way to a new generation. Yet Emily recently heard a friend sing this in a concert in Central Park; and in the midst of these strange times, some forty years after Dylan wrote it, this song was relevant again. Generation gaps are always unfolding but never in ways we can anticipate.

"What would the world be like," Emily asks, "if older generations delved into rebel youth music and the young rockers were opened to elements from the big band era?" It's intriguing. But perhaps, the two of us concluded, gaps are important. Without the tension of difference, music of any kind would never generate fresh ideas and styles. And think of the surprises we would miss.

Who knows when *Enigma Variations* or some other yet-to-be-heard piece will come storming into your life? Maybe it will resonate with your childhood, or maybe it will be utterly unfamiliar. It is wonderful to hear young Asian pianists and violinists who are passionate about

Mozart, wonderful to meet North Americans who are powerfully drawn to South American composers, or white suburban kids who can't get enough of the hip-hop streaming from black urban culture. We wonder: Is there a deep spiritual resonance given to human beings—a mysterious interconnection in and through music—that opens up our humanity to one another?

FINDING OUR MUSIC, FINDING OURSELVES

Listening to music and making music together help us find our place, our people, our selves. Searching for a way to belong, seeking to know who we are at the deepest level, is itself a spiritual search; and music accompanies us on this way. Emily observes, "We are made up of far more than we imagine. I discover parts of me by hearing what others sing, often in a different language." For both of us, this is a lifetime process and a mysterious goal. Listening, composing, performing, we half discover, half create our sense of who we are and where we belong.

The process is always in flux, because our musical tastes and loves change over time. Think of what you enjoyed hearing or performing when you were a teenager and what you now enjoy. "I still love the old stuff!" you might say. True. In listening to the old stuff, we realize where we've been and where we are headed. The power of music is to make us reflect on patterns in life, and sometimes nostalgia lures us back to hear the familiar over and over again. Sometimes that's exactly what we need—to hear again the music we connected with early on and to embrace again that part of our identity. In church there are times when it is really important to sing the old, old story. And the same thing happens at a rock concert, when fans call out to Amy and Emily, "Sing 'Galileo'!"—as if to say, this is part of our history with you. This happened again recently at Radio City Music Hall in New York; and nearly six thousand people, younger and older, sang with them. But change is also part of the story.

During his senior year in high school in 1955, Don was a disk jockey at a small-town Ohio radio station. "On one program I could play all my favorite records," he recalls: big bands like Count Basie, Billy May, Dave Brubeck, the unusual Sauter-Finegan band (with ninety different instruments), and Stan Kenton's milder songs (the station manager vetoed Kenton's wilder music). Nat King Cole and Doris Day, Sammy Davis Jr., the young Ella Fitzgerald, and the older Jo Stafford were the favored vocalists. "I still find all these musicians enjoyable," says Don, "but I have since done what all music lovers do: I have allowed new music to welcome me."

We need a musical home partly because it gives us a place from which to move on to new places. In junior high school, Emily loved John Denver's early songs. Then along came Patti Smith raging against the status quo, "and I could never quite go home again to the innocence of 'Rocky Mountain High.'" Think about it: all the songs and instrumental pieces people love were once new. This is true even of the most well-worn songs we learned from our grandparents. The golden oldies were once newly composed and had to be learned.

At the beginning of any life in music is love. People come to love music by listening and sharing it with others, by loving the people who love music. We learn to sing by singing—and never better than when we sing with people who love us and who also love music. This was certainly true for each of us.

When each of us took the next step and started to become a composer or songwriter, we were also basically joining in with others because we loved them and what they were doing musically. Emily remembers that when she first started writing, "I imitated songwriters, but most of my words were gibberish." She trots out the example of her first lyrics: "Didn't they know the people, didn't they know them well. Over forty thousand people, and they weren't doin' nothing wrong." Now we smile at these early attempts. As a young improviser on the piano, Don spent a lot of time memorizing blues styles straight out of a friend's book and imitating Louis Jordan's trio with his own high school group, called Three Guys Named Moe. Like other musicians before and after us, we learned from others, all the while searching for ways to make the music our own, a process that also was a way of coming into our own as persons.

Don remembers that when Emily was first taking group guitar lessons the instructor called out, "Who's playing that other stuff? Who's fooling around with those other chords?" She was already improvising, already searching for the new. Although our musical tastes and abilities have now become deep parts of our individual identities, each of us spent a long time searching for who we were musically. Even now various musical identities are often in tension, if not in conflict, inside us and between us. Sometimes our explorations have made us feel a bit like multiple personalities. But the real excitement has been—and still is—the sense that we are always on the edge of something new.

DISCOVERING A MUSICAL IDENTITY

Melva Costen, the gifted African American musician and editor of the *Presbyterian Hymnal,* tells of several trips to Africa she made with her late husband, James. The churches they visited in Kenya and elsewhere were singing and dancing in ways that literally enveloped the Costens with music. Worship there is permeated with song and movement, and music and community singing are natural parts of social life beyond worship as well. "I felt like I had come home to the music in my soul," Melva recalled in a conversation with Don. Deep African roots sounded within her, and she knew that she was part of this music. This music gave her a profound sense of belonging.

Melva Costen's experience reminds us that communal singing pervades daily life for many peoples in a way that is rare for most Americans. The distinctive spirituality of such societies or communities is carried by the music and especially by the body of song that continues from generation to generation. The American singer Paul Simon was drawn to this transgenerational spirituality. His recordings with the Ladysmith Black Mambazo singers from South Africa on *Graceland* and other albums tapped into a deep well of spiritual sound, making it accessible to millions of listeners outside Africa.

What is it in human life that cannot do without a song? The answer lies close to the heart of our identity. We sing out of who we have become as people, yet that singing can take on new forms as our identity and sense of belonging expand over time. We sing what we belong to and feel at home in. But we also sing in order to become part of a larger social reality. What some call spirituality—a way of being fully alive—is shaped by both of these pulls.

"Whatever people can say with passion and in heightened speech they will end up singing in some form," wrote Don in his chapter in *Practicing Our Faith,* a book that set the practice of "singing our lives to God" in the company of eleven other life-giving practices. "When language is used to move beyond the mere giving of information, we come to the threshold of song. When life is deeply felt or perceived, music gives shape and voice to the very pattern of our experienced world through pitch, rhythm, and intensity, through lyrics and harmony. The tensions, resolutions, moods, convictions, and playfulness of everyday life are translated into the patterns of sound." These facts about human beings and song help us understand how gaining a musical identity is part of our social bonding. Music forms us into communities from which we take, in large measure, our personal identity. Yet who we are and who we can yet be, as individuals and as communities, is also open to the songs we have yet to sing and hear.

Like some Aboriginal peoples of Australia, every people on earth has songlines. Specific experiences, places, and ideas need to be sung; and they are. Many people were surprised when the CD of distinctly American songs from the movie *O Brother, Where Art Thou?* became a big hit. But in the South, many people recognized familiar songlines. Hearing work songs alongside bluegrass and spirituals and country songs captured the atmosphere of a particular identity in the rural South of the 1920s and 1930s. That identity was social and religious, encompassing all facets of life—work, play, joy, sorrow.

When the ability to express such deep identity is suppressed, something is diminished. It was not surprising, then, that when the Soviets left the Baltic countries in 1989, one of the first acts of thousands of citizens was to sing in public. This was especially true in the small country of Estonia, which has long been known for its strong traditions of communal singing. When the Russian domination that Estonians had endured since the end of World War II came to an end, a quarter of a million people gathered to sing. A choir of twenty thousand voices came together in the stadium in Tallinn (now called the Singing Grounds) to sing a newly composed setting of the Mass, the worship service at the center of Catholic and other liturgical churches. Other music—especially music by their own composers—sounded throughout the city and the country. Imagine what it must have been like for those citizens to sing their national anthem publicly for the first time in fifty years! This dramatic example of the power of communal song came to be known as the singing revolution.

When Emily and Amy visited Cuba with other singer-songwriters in 1999, they were amazed at the street musicians in Havana. "They had so little to live on, but their music was so strong and life-giving," Emily remarked. "It's like their food and the air they breathe is song. Their rhythms and lines were so complex [that] we were in awe. When they asked us to join in, sometimes all Amy and I could do was clap our hands on simple beats." We both wondered about the way in which music has been so commercialized in the United States and whether there is anything like such a singing culture on these shores. Immediately, we thought of singing justice and freedom in the long history of African American music—a topic to which we will return in exploring music and justice.

The wider the range of music we come to appreciate, the broader our sense of life becomes. That is exactly how we, Emily and Don, have come to be who we are musically and who we are as persons in other ways as well, at this point in our lives—still exploring new aspects of what it means to be a woman, a man, of a particular cultural background, Americans, belonging to specific religious and spiritual traditions, citizens of the world.

Bringing a wider range of music into the church has been part of Don's work for many years. Emily said to him during the conversations leading up to this book:

> I've always appreciated the work that you, Dad, did during the years of committee meetings and discussions that went into preparing the *United Methodist Hymnal,* published in 1989. It includes hymns from many parts of the world: Asia,

Africa, Latin America. I like the language that is more inclusive of gender and of different cultures. This has changed my worship experience by making me feel welcomed by the words and music, sharing a global sense that connects me to far distant places and peoples. The strange and wonderful taste of a foreign melody deepens how I worship by taking me out of my own little world. Even if it is a cliché, celebrating diversity is part of the key to a heightened spirituality—the connection we discern between the personal and the universal. This is similar to the diversity we strive for in the secular world of music on tour: creating and participating in concerts that feature a variety of acts, actively seeking world music for its exotic yet solid connecting power. In both of our musical careers, we try musically to bridge the gaps between disparate communities.

SINGING OUR WAY TO NEW IDENTITIES

Music is not only an expression of identity; it can also allow a person to try on some imagined aspect of themselves. Even people who don't think of themselves as musical will sing in the shower or do their supposedly private versions of karaoke in their cars. Haven't we seen this—or done it ourselves—almost every day, especially when waiting for traffic lights? We asked our friend Tom why he loves to go to karaoke bars. "Because I can become a singer I admire, even if only for an evening." Tom speaks for many who enjoy the experience of taking on a musical personality vicariously. Who wouldn't like to sing as well as Frank Sinatra or Bonnie Raitt or Whitney Houston, if only for a night and without having to pay your dues and practice years of discipline as they did?

The popularity of karaoke intrigues us. Every weekend night thousands of wanna-be artists step up to a microphone and sing their hearts out with a recorded band. Some may just want to get a taste of performing, but others who have taken what the song expresses into themselves seem to want to share songs that have come to mean something to them; in a sense, they are offering a kind of testimony. When we were first writing this book, Don dismissed the phenomenon as a bit bizarre. But Emily kept saying that so many of her nonmusician acquaintances keep coming back to this kind of performance. Perhaps imitating famous singers allows them to try out different parts of their personalities.

A woman working at a local spa told Emily how she had always had a burning desire to sing in public, but she was quite timid and fearful. She said that she found karaoke bars both intimidating and enticing. Her son bet her that she wouldn't go "sing karaoke," but she finally worked up her courage, went by herself, and picked her song, a favorite of hers by the band Heart. When her turn came, she stepped quickly into the light, did her singing, and promptly fled the stage. Only then did she realize that the crowd was shouting encouragement. And that changed her. After that initial terrifying and exhilarating experience, she now goes whenever she can. Suddenly, she belongs to a whole community of singers who make music together in public and grow stronger as individuals in the process.

As we consider how music helps us to become someone new, we think also of a colleague of ours who has sung in an apparently quite different context: an accomplished church choir. As this choir has ventured out in recent years to sing a much wider range of choral music, he has become, he says, "a larger soul." We sensed what he means when we heard Emily's younger sister sing a wide range of choral pieces from all over the world and from many different periods of history with the exceptional choir at Marble Collegiate Church in Manhattan. Those outside the church may not realize that recent editions of many denominations' hymnals now incorporate songs and hymns from many cultures. Hymnals have reflected some diversity for a long time, but in recent decades the pace of change and the range of what they include have increased, because a majority of Christians worldwide are not European or North American but Asians and residents of the southern hemisphere. Now most denominational hymnals contain music in multiple languages, drawn from very different parts of the globe and reflecting the increasing diversity of the North American context as well. Thus, even ordinary congregations that sing from the hymnal over time find themselves trying on different musical identities. The first time Don led a largely white congregation in singing the Hispanic hymn *"Cuando el Pobre,"* he sensed that they were on the edge of growing into a new musical and theological aspect of their lives. The music is undeniably Latin American, and the text is like liberation theology set to music. (Liberation theology focuses on the relevance of Christian faith and life to situations of oppression and injustice, wherever in the world these are found.) "When the poor ones who have nothing share with strangers. . . . Then we know that God still goes that road with us."

Expanding musical boundaries is a challenge because at first it feels like you have to give up an identity that has become comfortable. It is easier for most people to sing what they know—in a sense, to sing what they have already become—than to venture into something new. Yet usually it does not take long to see that crossing musical boundaries is not a loss but a gain. When we try on the new, a broader vision of who we are and who we may yet become begins to dawn.

COMMUNITIES OF SONG, COMMUNITIES OF HOPE

How does music help us grow up and out of narrow ways of being who we are or who society assigns us to be? When talking about her high school and teenage years, Emily said,

> I remember how lonely my social experience was. Music was a kind of home, a place of safety. Almost everyone involved in the choir was on the fringe of popularity. There was so much peer pressure to be "in." The popular cliques set the tone for many of us. Chorus was one place where I fit in. In singing together we gained a special

89

Becoming Who We Are Through Music

identity; we were joined together in musical self-expression. Working for excellence was appreciated rather than put down by popular opinion. When the bell rang for the music period to begin, it was like a bell of freedom for me—a release from the classroom and hallway encounters I dreaded. I was walking into a room where we would join together to do something beautiful that took us out of our teenaged self-consciousness. We expressed our own artistic eccentricities too, but I grew more in chorus than anywhere else because the sound and language took me beyond myself—to a truer self. I became part of something much larger than my isolated self.

Emily's memories prompted similar thoughts for Don from fifty years ago. "I was not on the inside of the popular crowd either. Much of my early and middle teen years were lonely. Music was a refuge for some of us then as well. While playing violin and clarinet and singing in various music groups, I could forget that I did not run with the most popular students. Yet I also remember how proud the school was of our musical program." Both of us formed some of our deepest friendships in choir and other musical groups.

Music can both help us to find a defense against loneliness and allow us to express just how awfully lonely we are. Think of how many country songs are about loss of love and loneliness: "Only the Lonely," sang Ray Orbison, years before the Beatles' song "Eleanor Rigby" named the same melancholy reality. As a student Emily's sister Elizabeth often sang at an elder-care facility, where she tried to reach into the distinctive loneliness of old age with her singing. One of the friendships she made was with Margaret, then ninety-three years old. At Elizabeth's vocal recital at Oberlin, Margaret and several others from the facility came, most of them with walkers or in wheelchairs. After the recital's closing song, Margaret presented Elizabeth with roses. Another time, when Emily and her sisters sang "I'll Be Home for Christmas" at a nursing home, the older folks broke into tears. At first the sisters feared they had been insensitive, but later they realized how powerfully the song had worked to evoke a less lonely time for the audience.

When we talk with students in schools and colleges for whom music provided rescue from loneliness, they often mention the exciting nervousness of trying out for an ensemble, the shared discipline of rehearsals, the performance anxiety before a concert, and the surprising joy that comes with performing well. For many the classic moment was singing "You'll Never Walk Alone" at high school graduation—something both of us did in our different generations too! That song in that setting seemed to sum it all up, as sentimental as it now seems to us. Music helped name the loneliness and the struggle while at the same time helping us to overcome them. Singing together, we somehow forgot our self-preoccupation.

We wonder whether or in what ways it is different for most teens now. Do they also have the wonderful opportunities we enjoyed to overcome loneliness through music? When they don't have them in the communal settings of school and church, recorded music can sometimes be a friendly presence in their lives, offering a vicarious form of companionship. Time and time again, we have heard someone say, "I don't know what I would do without the songs I love." Don has talked to many older people who live alone but who find themselves listening to favorite hymns that provide company or to a favorite singer who once touched their hearts. Emily has heard from many a fan that a particular song has helped that person through a difficult time: "Love Will Come to You," "The Wood Song," or especially "The Power of Two." A favorite song or singer becomes a guide and a companion in this way for students in their dorm rooms or truck drivers sustained by the radio voices singing through the long night's journey. Listening, they feel themselves woven into a community.

"Growing up is hard to do," muses Emily, "but common music making might just hold a secret for us all." It's not just that music can lead us out of loneliness toward companionship. For good or for ill, we are deeply formed by musical experiences, especially when we become active participants in music making. Music shapes how we feel about life; and if we allow music in, it will continually open us up to new people, new experiences, new sounds. The discipline of trying to create something alive and beautiful together for others to hear creates a community. Friendships arise among the singers as well, after much time and energy spent together creating something bigger than our own self-preoccupations.

Music can be a balm for the lonely, but both of us discovered in those early years much more than comfort: we discovered a much broader world opening in and through the music making. You had to dig in and work hard. Others were counting on you. There was a built-in drive to do better. "Do your part, and do it well; above all listen to one another," we still hear our choir directors say. Would that we could live out that admonition in daily life.

"When we were all present, listening and trying our best to sing ensemble, it was magic," Emily recalled. "All the petty distinctions and the ego trips were left behind. The sound, the astounding sound that we made, and that those listening heard, moved us and our audience to new places." This is why, in a time when so many school systems are cutting their music programs, it is so important to fight for music. Vocal and instrumental groups are contexts of care, seedbeds, if not greenhouses, for a lifetime appreciation of music and for a richer experience of life in many other aspects as well. What would it be like if more kids of all ages in this country had such experiences? What new social solidarity might arise if whole generations could begin to sing and to enter into one another's song traditions? What would it be like if peoples of opposing nations could do this?

Perhaps it is becoming possible today to move outside our narrow identities in ways we could not have conceived of in the past. Emily and Amy have caught glimpses of this hope on many occasions. One memorable time was during the fall of the Berlin Wall in 1988–1989.

> We went to Berlin during the time the wall was coming down. We were shooting a video with the song "Get Together," a song espousing love for humanity; and we were donating the proceeds from that song to Habitat for Humanity. As we chipped away at that monolithic symbol of oppression, we thought of people coming

together to build houses and communities. So the song and the reality became a manifestation for me of divine work in the world: work to be done and how a song can fuel the fires of activism and social justice—when it created solidarity.

Emily brought back a piece of that wall. While we looked at it and felt it in our hands, Emily said, "I can almost hear the crowd joining in that singing and that solidarity, so rich in the promise of new freedom."

Music can lead us into all kinds of hopeful alliances. Emily treasures the times when music opens the way to connection and solidarity, especially when this happens across boundaries. A 1985 benefit concert for Atlanta's Our House, a homeless shelter for women and children, was one of these times. Suddenly, she realized "that to be able to give back at a grassroots level something of what I receive—this was powerful and real. It's interesting to me that I should have found that this is one of the things in our musical collaboration as the Indigo Girls that gives me the most satisfaction: singing benefit concerts that really make a difference in people's lives and in our own lives as well. Singing gives life a purpose when it is able to be for others. So our careers have included the joy of being able to play benefit concerts that support people working for a wide range of good causes." Don also thinks of his music as being offered and given away to the congregation in worship. Offered for the praise of God, it becomes also for the strengthening of the faith and hope and love of a community.

As we reflect on how music has helped each of us to develop personal identity and to be in solidarity with others, we realize that music has taught us to open our vulnerabilities and our hearts to others. To find out what these others are moved to feel, to see, to value, we ask: What music touches down in them? In us? What music has gathered experience from another generation or another culture than our own? In one sense, that is the question at the heart of this book and of Don and Emily's ongoing conversation: How can we practice crossing over appreciatively into music that is not immediately our own?

The question and the practice are hopeful. But there is also a dark side to the power of music that we will take up in the next chapter.

Chapter 6

MUSIC DIVIDES US

———

Take away from me the noise of your songs," thundered the prophet Amos nearly three thousand years ago; "I will not listen to the melody of your harps" (Amos 5:23). Amos meant this blast against the music of the hypocrites as an expression of God's own displeasure at their unfaithfulness. The anger in this passage may be a surprise after our previous discussions of the positive place of music in the Bible. Yet what it displays is a reality that casts a shadow over music throughout human communities. Music not only brings people together; it also pushes them apart. Sometimes the divisive point seems to be just a matter of taste; but sometimes musical divisions seem to reflect much bigger differences, differences about the meaning of what is good and bad that reach far beyond musical judgments.

An event at the Théâtre des Champs-Elysées in Paris on the evening of May 29, 1913, provides a helpful example. The occasion was the premier of *The Rite of Spring,* a new ballet with music by the Russian composer Igor Stravinsky that was eagerly anticipated because of the earlier success of *The Firebird,* a ballet that had also paired Stravinsky's music with the choreography of the famous dancer Vaslav Nijinsky. Yet this ballet was different; both the music and the dance violated most of the accepted conventions of the day. A few minutes into the performance, the well-dressed audience began to hiss and whistle disapproval. Unruly shouts soon erupted in the concert hall, and the performance was drowned out by the audience. Stravinsky's disturbing new music and the dancers' strange, sensuous, angular movements went against every norm of good music imaginable to the people in that audience. Their very musical identity was threatened in a way they sensed was somehow related to their overall personal and cultural identity as well.

Musical differences do not always cause riots. Yet almost every group that holds certain music dear might also, therefore, actively dislike other quite different music. This should be no surprise, given how formative music is for personal and communal identity. In this chapter we invite you to explore these divisions, in the hope of healing them or at least keeping them from doing greater harm.

MUSICAL TRIBES IN CONFLICT

At some basic level, musical taste is *tribal.* By this we mean that most people experience special bonding with others who prefer the same songs and music. "That's our kind of music!" some folks say with great passion—

implying, at the same time, "and that other music is not!" Both of us have encountered this pattern across the wide range of musical audiences each of us have engaged, from chamber music to rock concerts, in churches and schools, and on the street. Membership in a specific musical tribe—often one shaped also by ethnicity or economic class—becomes a badge of belonging. Thus, people whose tastes and convictions are formed by a specific sense of what sounds good may find new music disturbing. "We don't belong to that tribe," they implicitly say, just as the Parisians did with their booing in 1913.

Tom Troeger, a musician, scholar, and friend, tells of a sweet afternoon when he decided to leave his office and spend time in the park across the street. He was looking forward to listening to the sounds of spring—the birds, the wind in the trees, the splashing water in the fountain. But he remembers, "No sooner had I sat down than a young couple arrived carrying guitars. They began serenading each other with folk songs. A few minutes later, another couple settled on the grass behind me with a radio the size of a suitcase, which they had tuned to the local classical station. Then some college students came along and tossed a Frisbee to country western music. Finally, a van drove up and parked in front of me. It featured a bumper sticker: 'I'm a Hard Rocker.'" These colliding sounds drowned out the birds, wind, and water. "I felt surrounded by alien tribes: the folk tribe, the classical tribe, the country western tribe, and the hard rock tribe. Each group turned up its volume as the others arrived . . . so they did not have to listen to the competition." And Tom was surrounded by cacophony!

When a whole generation discovered rock 'n' roll in the 1950s and early 1960s, their parents were hard put to understand its appeal. And when Elvis Presley began to swing his hips to "You Ain't Nothin' but a Hound Dog," some immediately branded his music immoral. Don remembers his father reacting a few years later against Jimi Hendrix's wild guitar and Janis Joplin's hoarse, passionate singing—"It just sounds like so much screaming noise to me," he would say, turning off the car radio. Don realizes that his own initial, negative responses to Bob Dylan's "unpleasant" voice and to the heavy metal of Van Halen or to grunge were not so different. Don admits that at first he almost used the same words his father had used— "It is just so much noise"—and he confesses that he still has strong reactions to the intense sound levels many bands require in performance, including the Indigo Girls. Emily likes to point out all the ironies in these judgments, reminding Don how offensive his own father (her grandfather) found the wild arrangements of Stan Kenton's band when Don was totally caught up in them back in the 1950s and 1960s. "Why is it that I can take the high sound levels of Stravinsky's *The Rite of Spring* but can't quite take that heavy metal sound?" Don wonders aloud. Quality and artistry, some folks would say, are what make the difference. But given the prejudices that have emerged in history and in our own lives, we are not sure that's the whole story. And so the debate over new music continues.

More than new music or high decibel levels, the associations people have with specific kinds of music are often at the heart of their disagreements and debates. For example, some church people have reacted very strongly against the use of blues and jazz forms in worship. In the late 1960s, Don sometimes played jazz in a church coffee-house. This was fine with the church members—until he added a bit of jazz to a Sunday service. The first time they took some of those jazzy hymn arrangements into the sanctuary, some people were turned off, he recalls. "That music belongs in a bar, not in church!" exclaimed one older white man who belonged to the church. The associations he brought to blues and jazz were just too strong to allow him to think of this music as religious. The sounds evoked dark, smoky places where people were up to no good. Yet in African American churches during that time, Don often got quite another response. Duke Ellington's piece "Come Sunday," when played in St. James Freewill Baptist Church or the Cathedral of St. John the Divine in New York, fit right in. In fact, because much African American church music has resonated with blues and jazz, in some contexts these musical forms did not carry negative associations at all. Such music deepens worship because it is connected to real life. Both of us have worshiped in some congregations in the black tradition that might find Ellington passé and whose members prefer commercial gospel music in worship. While some embrace such forms, other congregations prefer the older forms of hymns and the traditional spirituals.

An African American student friend, BeSean Jackson, says that many of the younger generation in his church consider the "old-timey" spirituals and songs unappealing because they are too full of sorrow and suffering. "I was raised in the church on the older traditions of song, which still mean so much to me, but I can see the reason why so many of my friends don't like to sing things like 'and he never said a mumbalin' word' or 'nobody knows the trouble I've seen.'" The younger people, by and large, want something more positive and affirming. The deep memories and associations are painful; the newer upbeat gospel music is full of life and self-esteem. BeSean feels the conflict in himself too: he shares part of his peers' desire to avoid the sad words and slower melodies of lament, but he also realizes that these older songs carry the memories of what his forbears really experienced—a history of suffering and courage, adversity and profound hope.

In spite of this debate within himself and within his community, BeSean also recognizes a positive aspect of musical tribalism. As a minority student in a predominantly white university, he finds strength in the distinctive music of his own cultural group. "Sometimes I can't wait to get to my car and turn on the music that reminds me of my own roots. It empowers me, keeps me going." In this sense, the music of the tribe can be a positive force. It becomes destructive only when one tribe says to another, "Your songs are inferior." When this happens, it is possible that stereotyping and generalizing about whole groups of people and their music are masking conflicts that are really based not on music but on deeper human prejudices. In such cases music becomes the bearer of ideologies, fracturing community rather than enhancing it.

It is hard to sing other people's songs when we share nothing of life with them. Thus, when people don't really know one another, the fact that they like different kinds of music can become the symbol of other kinds of differences—cultural, moral, and religious. The irony is that when you hear someone saying, "I will not listen to that junk," you could equally well be hearing a rocker who thinks classical music is boring and elitist or an operagoer who disdains all forms of popular music.

Judgments and refusals to listen that are this sweeping, we want to suggest, don't come from a mere difference in taste. Rather, they are likely to emerge when people fear that somehow those who belong to a different musical tribe threaten their fundamental beliefs about human beings, their own history, and how they choose to live. When this happens, clashes of culture are disclosed as clashes of identity; and here music can mark deep and dangerous divisions.

"Some people are vehement in their distaste for rap music," Emily says.

> But whenever someone is borderline vitriolic about not liking music, I think there is something deeper going on than simply taste. When people say, "I hate that music," they are really saying, "I hate that culture." Of course, some rap music is full of posturing, sexism, and the pursuit of material things. But is that any different from white rock 'n' roll hair bands [so called because of their big, teased-out hairstyles] from the eighties who had women laid out across cars as they sang the virtues of sex, drugs, and rock 'n' roll?
>
> Many people miss the integrity and power of rap music when they dismiss it with generalizations about all such musicians. To know Public Enemy's rap, for example, is to get in on the real story of the political and economic oppression of

blacks. To know Tupac Shakur's rap is to know the story of a young black male, growing up on violent streets, trying to do more than survive, expressing his identity through words and music. His language is poetic, fierce, and brilliantly woven to the beat. The sound samples used in his tracks trace histories of music and create new hybrids. No one really knows what it's like unless one shares that life. Yet artists like Tupac, Notorious B.I.G., Public Enemy, and Queen Latifah—to name a few—provide some of the deepest insights into the social realities of black urban life, with all its beauty, pain, and hardship.

I sometimes see the same reaction to country music. A would-be listener shuts down because of the perceived generalizations about country culture: it's all conservative; it's all redneck or all unsophisticated bumpkin stuff. We should fight against our impulses to generalize about people and music. In my mind, some of the most beautifully crafted and moving songs are country songs—songs with amazing, subtle attention to melody and turns of phrase.

In Whitesburg, Kentucky, a center called Appalshop is developing a program called From the Holler to the Hood. Working with poets and musicians, some of whom are in prisons, they bring hip-hop and Appalachian artists together to write music. This seems to be one of those places where true understanding of one another's culture does open up, as wildly different communities of musicians begin to create new and challenging song. Anything is possible when people come together with open minds, to listen and grow by taking in the stories of cultures other than their own. Music offers access to these precious things. When shared in such a way, rather than causing a battle, music makes possible an opening up of identity.

USED OR ABUSED?

Music always carries deep powers of association. Think of the powerful cultural memories a song can evoke. "God Bless America" aroused many people to pride in the United States during World War II; and in the days following September 11, it was used to recall that pride and to invoke divine assistance for the United States during another dangerous time. In a very different way, TV ads use the stereotyped association of classical music with the upper crust to add an aural dimension to the images of luxury cars or jewelry they are trying to sell. It is as if advertisers think that the music of the Italian composer Antonio Vivaldi sounds like the driver of an expensive car feels.

A more severe problem of association is found when music is manipulated to serve cruel purposes. A shocking example appears in Stanley Kubrick's 1971 film *A Clockwork Orange,* when beautiful music becomes a trigger for violence through a process of brainwashing. In real life the Nazis used music deliberately and powerfully in their propaganda, both through marching songs that energized youth brigades preparing for World War II and through the extensive use of music in their rallies and films. In the opening scene of *Triumph of the Will,* an influential 1936 film by Leni Riefenstahl, Adolph Hitler's plane descends from the heavens through beautiful clouds to music from *Tannhäuser,* an opera by the nineteenth-century German composer Richard Wagner. The music gives the scene immense quasi-religious power. As it turned out, association works in both directions. Although the propagandists were trying to promote Hitler by associating him musically with the mythic heroes in Wagner's operas, one result was to bestow a lingering Nazi association on Wagner's music. Francis Ford Coppola's 1970s Vietnam film *Apocalypse Now* made use of this association by linking Wagner's "Ride of the Valkyries" to ominous swooping helicopters moving in to kill. And disputes about whether and how people might again receive the beauty of Wagner's music in a post-Holocaust world have continued for more than half a century.

When music gets used for cruel purposes, the conflict and divisions of musical tribalism reach an unacceptable and even lethal level. The two of us are less certain what to make of using music to serve blatantly commercial purposes. Both of us are aware of how TV commercials consciously exploit music in order to sell products—a reality so omnipresent that most Americans just take it for granted. An earlier generation was raised on commercial jingles, from "Light Up a Lucky" to "See the USA in your Chevrolet," while more recent patterns feature the use of classical music to sell luxury items and rock music to promote the NFL. Most of the time, we think nothing of this and even allow ourselves to be mildly entertained by such uses of music. Yet we are also wary of how advertisers try to weave associations between music and their products that will endure long beyond the end of the commercial itself. When music is used in an effort to transform the authentic religious enthusiasm inherent in such music into enthusiasm for a particular product, we suspect that use is giving way to abuse.

WORSHIP WARS

Today music is at the heart of another war—though here, fortunately, that is just a metaphor. It also plays an important role in a debate about how to attract those who are "shopping" for a church—also, we hope, a metaphor. This is a conflict raging in congregations of nearly every denomination about the style of worship and especially about what music is suitable. Should Christians who gather for worship sing the same hymns their grandparents did, accompanied by an organ? Should they seek out music from other cultures that will challenge them to expand their horizons and change their image of the church? Should they put down their hymnals, lift up their hands, and sing only simple songs whose words are projected on a screen and whose melodies are led by a rock band? These debates about music are a crucial aspect of a huge revisioning in styles of worship that is raging across the church. As Don's colleague Thomas Long writes in his recent book *Beyond the Worship Wars,* "Rare is the congregation that has not felt some stress, some measure of conflict, over all this ferment in worship."

Sometimes controversy focuses on a single hymn.

This happened in the late 1980s when Don and some colleagues were working on a new hymnal for the United Methodist Church. The editor in chief, Carlton Young, recalls that some committee members were concerned that some older hymns' language seemed too narrow or exclusive. They worked successfully to relieve the predominance of male language about human beings and to alter and enrich language about God. But as the committee members debated changing or even dropping certain hymns, they began to receive protests from many church members, whose opinions they really did want to hear. As it turned out, the biggest controversies really emerged over military imagery; when the group considered dropping "Am I a Soldier of the Cross?" for example, the protest mail poured in.

However, nothing prepared the committee for the torrent that followed its eleven-to-ten vote to delete "Onward Christian Soldiers," a hymn that pictures Christians "marching as to war." Some love this hymn because it seems to them to provide a faithful endorsement of Christian civic and national duty; others appreciate it as a rousing metaphorical call to spiritual dedication in resisting evil; others oppose it because they worry that it has militaristic overtones that work against peace. As some within the church began to criticize the deletion of this highly singable old standard, all the television networks picked up the story. ABC sent a crew to interview Mr. Young, and another network interviewed a young African American Methodist man who happened to be standing outside the U.S. Supreme Court in Washington and who lamented, "I wish they hadn't done that." The open process the committee had set up to receive suggestions through opinion sessions throughout the church turned for the most part into angry, foot-stomping, shouting matches between the pros and cons. By the time of its next meeting, the committee had received over eleven thousand letters, only forty-four of which supported the deletion! The committee restored the hymn. But a deep division had surfaced in this early battle in the worship wars.

In 2004, Don did a weekend workshop in a local church that was badly split over the question of music and especially over what can be considered appropriate for worship. On one side was a group consisting mostly of longtime members who wanted to sing the old-time music. Hymns like "How Great Thou Art" or "Blessed Assurance," they complained, were not included in worship services any more. Another group wanted the hymns and songs selected for congregational singing to challenge them. They were interested in hymns that spoke honestly of suffering, pain, or doubt—including some of the most complex older hymns, such as Martin Luther's "A Mighty Fortress Is Our God" and Charles Wesley's "Love Divine, All Loves Excelling." A third group didn't like either of the first two approaches. They wanted short, lively, praise choruses driven by more rhythmic elements provided by drums and an electric keyboard. "Why can't we do away with the hymnals and project the words on screen?" they kept asking. Yet another group longed for more contemplative and meditative music and song. They favored music from the Taizé community or the songs of John Bell from the Iona Community in Scotland.

The existence of these very different viewpoints within a single congregation illustrates the tremendous impact of the availability of many varieties and styles of music in the larger culture on the church. More and more churches experience these tensions. Indeed, when these tensions become very strong, many congregations break into enclaves of music taste that worship separately at different worship services, each with its own musical flavor. In the most difficult cases, as with the church Don just mentioned, strong feelings and prejudices have emerged, and the unity of the whole is threatened.

"What language shall I borrow, to thank thee, dearest friend?" asks a hymn attributed to the twelfth-century monk Bernard of Clairvaux that worshipers still sing in many churches today. This question, which the hymn addresses to Christ, expresses the inadequacy of our human words—and we might add of our human songs—to express our deepest spiritual realities. And yet in the worship wars, it is as if everything hangs on musical styles and whether the words are familiar or sung with a beat. The irony for both of us is, of course, that all language about God is limited; the divine reality requires a wide range of music if we even begin to express our awe and wonder. The conflicts will be deep and divisive as long as people do not listen to one another in love. Each faction needs to try much harder to understand why certain music and song is meaningful to those with whom they disagree.

Emily has also experienced stylistic clashes when

making music. Her recollections of musical disagreement when she and Amy are working on a record (and how it gets resolved) is another version of the clash.

> I can remember recently arranging songs with the band, and our producer suggested using a swing feel for one of the songs I had written. We played it and played it again using this approach, and while I tried to accept this direction largely because we have a talented producer whose ideas are usually great, I found myself unable to assimilate that style and feel its appropriateness for the song. My body had an almost visceral reaction against it. There are many times when Amy and I try a new stylistic approach to a song, and it takes getting used to before we realize it was a good change to make from the original arrangement. But in this case, we simply abandoned the song because we couldn't make it work together in a way that was soul satisfying. I may not have it in me to write and perform a swing song, even though I appreciate that style in many other artists. Sometimes when I am trying to create a part for one of Amy's songs, she may feel it is too pretty, and I may feel her ideas are too edgy. But in the end, our music is made more interesting by the sometimes undetectable intersection of different styles.

What paths might lead through and beyond musical conflicts? Finding them will depend on our willingness to listen and our openness to new thinking about what we hear, sing, and play.

Beyond the Clash

It is intriguing that an ancient letter about love uses musical imagery to describe the nature of conflict and spiritual inauthenticity. "If I speak in the tongues of mortals and of angels, but do not have love, I am a noisy gong or a clanging cymbal" (1 Corinthians 13:1). Today in the midst of clashing musical symbols, the two of us want to encourage everyone who loves music to learn to practice respect for the dignity of musical differences. We need to confront our prejudices. But we also need to hold on to what we know is strong and good music. Some music does take us more deeply into life than does other music, and there are reasons for this. We must make musical judgments but not in a judgmental manner.

This approach to musical difference is especially likely to take hold when it is framed by a respectful relationship between two people who like each other but dislike each other's music. The two of us want to share our own experience as an example. However, we believe that others also have relationships that can help them to transcend musical divisions: parents, sons and daughters; those who belong to the same church; those who work together; or just friends. But you have to be willing to listen closely—to your conversation partner and also to the music that he or she loves.

Here is how it sometimes goes between the two of us.

DON: The problem with so much commercial pop music is that it is based on musical clichés without any sense of irony.

EMILY: Be careful here. It is too easy to sneak in our class
         and social attitudes, and sometimes these are
         explicitly ethnic and racial.

Or

EMILY: I don't have much patience to listen to some of the
         avant-garde abstract concert music. I may find it
         interesting, but it doesn't move my soul.

DON: Be careful here. Some of that abstract music may
         actually contain some of the same elements you
         love in jazz—say in the wild patterning of notes
         in John Coltrane's sax.

And then we begin to point things out to one another. And
sometimes we do persuade each other to hear and appreciate things we could not have heard without one another's
help. So we attend in order to avoid our own stereotypes
and generalizations about "that kind" of music for which
we at first have no perception, let alone taste.

We both see encouraging signs that people can not
only get beyond musical divisions but even learn to appreciate them for the diversity they provide. Emily says, "One
of the highlights of my career has been the Lilith Fair tour,
a traveling festival of women musicians and their bands.
We played to sold-out venues. Both the musicians and the
audience really enjoyed the diverse variety of women
artists, from country to hip-hop and everything in between." Don takes encouragement from the many classically trained musicians who are also good at jazz or in
popular music. He knows several symphony players who
really enjoy rhythm and blues and other nonclassical
music on their days off. Discovering that different kinds
of music give different kinds of pleasure, for players and

listeners alike, can be a most enjoyable discovery, especially when your tastes have been very narrow. What really impresses us both, however, is how the history of music, sacred and secular, popular and classical, keeps surprising us with cross-influences. Great musicians in any musical genre seem to have wide radar—a crossover range and versatility that keeps challenging our categories.

Of course, each of us still has some favorite music and a few very favorite songs, though the favorites might shift depending on who we are with and what situation we are in. In this we are like almost everybody: we have favorites, and we will probably continue to play favorites and allow our appreciation for a particular artist or composer to grow even deeper over time. But we want also to respect and be open to artists beyond these and invite others to do the same. Becoming too narrow in your taste—and especially claiming that your own music is superior—means letting music divide you from others more than is good for you or for the world. And it also means missing out on some really great music you might never have heard in your lifetime.

A Song to Sing, A Life to Live

Chapter 7

SINGING
OUR SORROW

———

Grief comes to all of us sooner or later. And when it does, according to an old Yiddish teaching cited by Rabbi Abraham Joshua Heschel, we undergo three levels of mourning. The first is tears. The second is silence. The third is song.

One of the most powerful songs that expresses that third level is an old spiritual that we have heard sung in a such a way that all the suffering of the world seems to be expressed in the singing.

> Sometimes I feel like a motherless chile,
> Sometimes I feel like a motherless chile,
> Sometimes I feel like a motherless chile,
> a long way from home, a long way from home.
> Sometimes I feel like a mournin' dove . . .
> Sometimes I feel like a moanin' dove . . .
> Sometimes I feel like a mornin' dove . . .

The melody and the words go directly to the lonely, abandoned heart.

For all the joy and delight music can bring, we also know that it can sound our losses and our grief. Some music can carry us into the depths, to places of honesty and eventually healing. On rare occasions this kind of music has compelled both of us to face the truth of how we feel when perhaps we would rather not. Music has exposed our wounds, named our losses, and made us cry. Yet we have also been consoled, comforted, and healed by song.

EXPOSING THE WOUNDS

Grief is one of the deepest and most complex emotions human beings can experience. Sometimes it is tinged with anger, sometimes with sheer rage, and sometimes it is one long sob. Some of us have known grief as sheer numbness or sustained depression. The death of a child, a parent, a sister, a brother, a partner; the loss of a dear friend or even a beloved pet—each of these brings its own peculiar weave of feeling, mood, behavior, thought. Grief also comes when we ponder the immense suffering human violence causes in our world today. It is hard to take in the loss of so many innocent children caught in the cross fire of war not of their making.

If you have ever grieved deeply over loss, you know how the world seems to change around you. A whole range of emotions moves through and around you, whether or not you go through particular stages of mourning. You are at your most tender and vulnerable. This is a place to which music can come.

When Emily's younger sister died unexpectedly in 1999, we kept saying "I can't believe she's gone." Music was one of our primary ways of coming to terms with her death. As a family we often had sung together, whether in the car on trips, around the piano at home, or in church. We could all remember Carrie singing a pure melody line while her sisters harmonized, until the whole family was singing along.

When a large congregation gathered at Carrie's funeral, we who so missed her voice were suddenly surrounded by hundreds of voices singing strong hymns of consolation and thanksgiving.

> O God, our help in ages past, our hope for years to
>   come,
> our shelter from the stormy blast, and our eternal
>   home!
> Time, like an ever rolling stream, bears all who breathe
>   away;
> they fly forgotten, as a dream dies at the opening day.
>
> O God, our help in ages past, our hope for years to
>   come,
> be thou our guide while life shall last, and our eternal
>   home.

In the midst of all these voices, we sang lament, the song of loss and sorrow. Yet at the same time, we also sang doxology, the song of thanks and praise, for Carrie's life. The two mingled together in a mysterious way.

Like so many teens and twenty-somethings, Carrie was fond of putting her favorite songs together on a cassette tape. Sometimes she put crazy and wonderful pieces side by side: Nine Inch Nails came right after Mozart. You can imagine what it was like to listen again in her absence to some of those tapes. All the range of who she was sounded in and through those songs. The music she chose was part of who she was. Our family's ongoing process of grieving and healing is now forever woven into those words and melodies.

Emily's response included composing a song.

> After Carrie's death, everything in my life changed. It was a strange mix of almost unbearable pain at times and a deepening of daily experience that was marked by personal growth: colors became more vivid, breezes more soothing, my tears bigger, my laughter heartier. The unmistakable presence of her spirit loomed and stayed with me as I struggled with the physical loss of her life. I turned to music to help me speak these things. The result was a song called "She's Saving Me." That song is more than a bare remembrance of Carrie. When I sing it, she comes back to me and is with me. That song evokes Carrie for me. This is when I know that music can be a spiritual gift and that it has the power to bring to life those who have passed through death. So with music I am never really alone. It links me to all other realms, whatever they may be. Death loses its sting in the presence of truly evocative music.

MUSIC AND PUBLIC TRAGEDY

Every January the city of Atlanta commemorates Dr. Martin Luther King Jr. week, remembering both the birthday and the assassination of a prophet who grew up in and later ministered in that city. Even as time bears us away farther from this loss each year, echoes of anguish continue to fill the city at that time, some of it expressed in song. But these echoes are mingled with a renewal of hope for the justice Dr. King proclaimed. When singing "We Shall Overcome," the two of us still feel the dream deferred, but we are also stirred to hope. This song has this effect on us not only in Atlanta but also in other cities, at other times.

Mysteriously, music can do more than touch our sorrow. It can also take us the next step, embracing us with strange comfort and sometimes even healing. We have been amazed by the way it has sometimes made shared grieving possible far beyond the bounds of family or religious community. Don recalls the playing of Samuel Barber's "Adagio for Strings" in the days after President John F. Kennedy's assassination. Then it was played again on the radio in the days following September 11. This particular piece of music captures the curve of great sadness, helping those who hear it to bear unspeakable loss. The ambiguous opening harmonies, the quiet intensity of the strings, the unfolding tensions, the rise and fall of pitches—all of these gave a form to feelings that were too huge to comprehend, in the process providing a mirror for our own experience. Barber's "Adagio" seems to get inside the contours of grief.

A remarkable story of music and the trauma of September 11, 2001, is recounted in Barry Green's book *The Mastery of Music*. Many in New York wanted to help in the terrible crisis, and Juilliard School of Music offered to send a string quartet to provide music at the Armory—

a vast military building to which rescue workers returned after their shifts and where many gathered to await news of missing loved ones. William Harvey, a young violin student, was one of the volunteers. He described his experience in a letter he sent to friends in Indiana; but it was soon on the Internet, being read by millions around the globe.

> Yesterday, Sept. 15, I had probably the most incredible and moving experience of my life. . . .
>
> Entering the building was very difficult emotionally, because the entire building (the size of a city block) was covered with missing persons posters. Thousands of posters, spread out up to eight feet above the ground, each featuring a different, smiling, face.
>
> I made my way into the huge central room and found my Juilliard buddies.
>
> For two hours we sight-read quartets (with only three people!), and I don't think I will forget the grief counselor from the Connecticut State Police who listened the entire time, or the woman who listened to "Memory" from the Broadway play *Cats,* crying the whole time.

When Harvey's fellow musicians had to leave, he volunteered to play solo. A military officer asked him to play for his soldiers, who were returning from the terrible work at Ground Zero.

> So at 9 P.M., I headed up to the second floor as the first men were arriving. From then until 11:30 P.M., I played everything I could do from memory: Bach B Minor Partita, Tchaikovsky's violin concerto, the Dvorak concerto, Paganini Caprices

1 and 17, Vivaldi's "Winter" and "Spring," the theme from *Schindler's List,* Tchaikovsky's "Melodie," "Meditation" from *Thaïs,* "Amazing Grace," "My Country 'Tis of Thee," "Turkey in the Straw," "Bile Them Cabbages Down."

Never have I played for a more grateful audience. Somehow it didn't matter that by the end, my intonation was shot and I had no bow control.

I would have lost any competition I was playing in, but it didn't matter.

It turned out that he was playing for the men of the Fighting Sixty-Ninth, one of the most decorated divisions in the U.S. Army. In a rare gesture of thanks, their colonel presented him with the coin of the regiment bearing the insignia of the Fighting Sixty-Ninth. Afterward, riding the taxi uptown to Juilliard, Harvey felt numb. "Not only was this evening the proudest I've ever felt to be an American, it was my most meaningful as a musician and a person as well."

William Harvey reflects at the end of the letter, "Next time I want to get into a petty argument about whether Richter or Horowitz was better, I'll remember that when I asked the colonel to describe the pit formed by the tumbling of the towers, he couldn't. Words only go so far, and even music can only go a little further from there."

In this story the power of music to speak to human beings in the midst of deep suffering is clear. Music goes beyond what can be spoken. It exposes the wound, yes, but in a way that may in time begin the process of healing. Other musicians also made offerings near Ground Zero in those dark days, among them Yo-Yo Ma and Renee Fleming. Again and again music reached into parts of human experience about which it was impossible to speak, touching the most tender center of life. The wondrous mélange of material Harvey offered—everything he knew by heart—came as a surprising gift for men and women exhausted by literal grief work.

SINGING A LOVED ONE HOME

"There is some music I would never play as easy listening or as background music," a friend and student of Don's observed. "I need time and a place to give myself to it—especially music that touches the deep places." He is so right. Some music forces us to confront places in our inner life that we did not even know we had. This kind of music demands our full attention.

One example is *"Kindertotenlieder"* (songs on the death of children), by the great Austrian composer Gustav Mahler. *"Kindertotenlieder"* is heartbreaking in its subject, in its composition, and in its live performance. Mahler set five poems of Friedrich Ruechert (1788–1866) that portray a father grieving over the deaths of two young children. The interplay of the solo voice and the instruments portray the isolation and aloneness of personal grief in the midst of the life of nature, which continues quite indifferent to the father's anguish. The music also communicates what one commentator calls "a hammering anxiety that half believes that it still must be possible to do something about the situation, and a ferocious guilt that strikes again and again because the children are being destroyed and nothing is being done about it."

Sarah Woolf was a vibrant teenager entering her senior year at Decatur High School in suburban Atlanta when she developed Ewing's sarcoma, a virulent type of bone cancer. She was a wonderful student, an outgoing friend to many, and had been nurtured in a strong and musical Christian family. She sang and played guitar, and among her favorite pieces of music were several songs by the Indigo Girls. At first hopes rose when she went into remission, but then her cancer returned. By the time of her graduation, it was clear that the cancer was terminal. Her family and high school friends surrounded her with care and near the end provided hospice care at home.

One of Sarah's favorite songs was Emily's "Southland in the Springtime," a song Sarah continued to play and sing even in the later stages of her illness. When Amy and Emily returned from a tour, they learned of Sarah's situation and came to her bedside to sing for her, even though she appeared to have slipped from consciousness. Just a few hours after their visit, Sarah died peacefully.

Her parents asked Emily to sing at Sarah's funeral at Oakhurst Baptist Church. Emily recalls sitting in the front pew with Don and waiting to sing. "I really wondered how I might get through 'Southland in the Springtime.' Somehow I did, and because she loved the song and used to play and sing it herself, it was like I had named her in the music." With the song as a witness, we sang a loved one home.

After playing several funerals with Amy over the last few years, Emily has become aware of how music can link the living and the dead. In one case, at the service for a community leader who had been killed in a tragic accident, Emily sang "Fare Thee Well My Bright Star"—not because it was the woman's favorite, but because it captured the community's admiration of her. After the unexpected death of another friend, they offered a folk ballad, "The Water Is Wide," in a simple style, with the voices in close harmony.

As a church organist, Don has played many a funeral service. Over the years he has constantly been struck by how those planning the service always try to include one or more of the deceased person's favorite songs. Often in the South, the music is a wondrous mixture of old-time gospel songs and complex classic hymns like "For All the Saints Who from Their Labors Rest." To prepare his students for the funerals they will themselves play, Don often asks them to prepare their own funeral as a final project for the term. Most soon realize that deciding what hymns and other music to include is crucial and that the songs, hymns, psalms, and anthems they include should help those who are gathered both to name the loss and to be strengthened in the faith of the church. The students often end up asking friends who are not in the class what music they would choose for their own funerals. Though responses to this question vary, those who ponder it recognize that the music shared at such a time serves both to express grief and to affirm faith in the face of death. Appropriate choices help those who mourn to be honest about naming their losses and bereavements, whereas poor choices can rob them of a crucial aspect of the grieving process. Such music, sung in the face of the mystery of life and death, brings spiritual consolation.

"NOBODY KNOWS THE TROUBLES I'VE SEEN . . ."

"Out of the depths I cry to you, O Lord. Lord, hear my voice!" The Hebrew Psalms are full of laments such as this one from Psalm 130. To *lament* means to pour out your sorrows, to mourn out loud. Psalm 88, perhaps the darkest of all, is in the voice of one who pleads and complains day and night because God seems so absent: "You have caused friend and neighbor to shun me; my companions are in darkness" (verse 18). Even some who have read the Bible all their lives are surprised to learn that there are more psalms of lament than any other kinds of psalms, including those that offer thanks and praise to God. Perhaps we aren't ready to notice them before we need them. The psalms of lament seem to lie in wait for us, ready to provide language when we are visited by pain and suffering.

In a different way, the blues also give voice to lament. Both of us play blues, Emily on guitar, Don on piano. Much of the blues is a musical cry, with origins in suffering and oppression experienced in the daily lives of African Americans. As someone once explained to Emily, "The blues is what you get when life ain't right." In listening closely we come to hear the connections between

Singing Our Sorrow

many spirituals and the blues. Both forms of song are ways of coping and living with pain and misery. The religious sentiment in the old spiritual "He Never Said a Mumbalin' Word"—"They crucified my Lord, and he never said a mumbalin' word"—is expressed in a sad swooping melody and a slow tempo close to those the great blues singer Bessie Smith used in many of her songs. The only way to live with the blues is to sing them.

The American blues singer Billie Holiday recorded one of the most haunting songs of lament to come out of the experience of racism. The words, written in 1937 by Abel Meeropol, a Jewish schoolteacher in New York, confront the listener with an unbearable set of images:

> Southern trees bear strange fruit
> Blood on the leaves and blood at the root
> Black bodies swinging in the Southern breeze
> Strange fruit hanging from the poplar trees.

This lament on lynching still evokes a shudder. Billie Holiday's voice moaned and wept in the singing, responding to one of our nation's greatest sorrows.

Not all blues songs address traumas this overwhelming. Many sing of the losses and griefs that can happen to anyone—broken love affairs, misunderstanding, deception, and the blues in the night. Life's melancholy is nowhere else so immediately sounded. Both of us have found improvising blues music to be a helpful way of working through our own emotional responses to pain, Emily with guitar and voice, Don with piano or organ. We lament and grieve over many things—lost chances, broken relationships, injustice, others' pain, and loneliness—and in doing so, we find that music not only exposes the wounds but also helps us to identify our sorrow and confront what aches in us.

Although Emily and Don do not always respond equally to all country music, it is obvious to both of us that this music tells the story of many people's lives. It's the sung story that draws people in—"Hank Williams, Emmylou Harris sing about things that happen in my life," a friend of ours explained. From the mountains we also hear lament and the pain of struggle and hurt in the folk song traditions of Appalachia, many of which draw on biblical images.

> I'm just a poor, wayfarin' stranger
> Travelin' through this world of woe;
> But there's no sickness, no toil or danger,
> In that bright world to which I go.
> I'm going there to see my (mother, father)
> I'm going there, no more to roam,
> I'm just a going over Jordan,
> I'm just a going over home.

Life in the mountains working in the mines was typically hard and fleeting, possessing a pathos that can be heard in the untrained voices of singers from the mountains. A sense of mortality hangs in the melancholy melodies and sometimes dark lyrics.

THE TRANSFORMING POWER OF SONG

"A song is a gift musicians can give to the bereaved," says Emily. Even though the gift of music in human extremity can seem to stir up the pain, it can also console, comfort, and even transform us. The psalms of Hebrew and Christian Scriptures reflect this reality. As we have noted, they voice lament in strong words. Yet many also move on beyond pain, to remember the past goodness of God, to give thanks, and to return the singer to life. In the opening lines of Psalm 13, the speaker cries out to God from the pain in his soul, the sorrow in her heart, "How long? Will you forget me forever?" By the psalm's end, the speaker remembers having trusted God's "steadfast love" in the past and realizes that once again in the future, "I will sing to the Lord," whose grace and care have been bountiful.

George Dennison's beautiful yet terrifying short novel, *Luisa Domic,* provides a vivid image of music's power to heal. The title character has escaped from the aftermath of the bloody overthrow of President Allende's 1970s government in Chile, but she is still tormented by visions of the inhuman brutality she witnessed there. She comes as a political refugee to Maine, where she is received into a household that loves music and poetry. Increasingly disturbed by what her hosts cannot possibly know of her previous experience, she finally breaks down, screaming uncontrollably. The children are terribly frightened, and her hosts have no idea what to do. But their musician friend, Harold, sits down at the piano and begins to play

> an imitation of Luisa's voice. Its notes were similar; it pushed where her screams simply endured; it dropped to a lower register and pulsed more quietly while she gasped for air. I had seen Harold do exactly this with the disturbed children. . . .

128

Luisa was braced in that kneeling position, holding the sides of her face and staring straight ahead. Her entire body shook when she screamed, and swelled like a bellows when she grasped for air. . . . One heard many notes in her voice, a hoarseness that conveyed the pain of her throat, notes of terror that were chilling to hear, and still others that expressed unbelief or outrage. . . . No instrument could have expressed all this as her voice expressed it Harold contrived equivalents . . . . . . Where we others had . . . . . . er, to bring her back to no . . . . . . d gone out to her and fou . . . . . . It was this music, really . . . man presence beside her i . . . . . . ave thought would be an . . . . . . ness of agony. That presence could do nothing, or little, about her agony, or about the outrage of the soul; nevertheless is *was* a presence, and it said persistently, *I am with you, I am with you.*

Gradually, Luisa is brought to the end of her sobbing and to a new quiet, present in her own body again. So the music "sang to her a full, very quiet song. . . . It was as if the sufferer and her guide had emerged from the underground into a little grove where sunlight shone among trees and bushes, and the sufferer sat with bowed head, grieving silently, and the guide sang gravely in his own solitude beside her." Harold's incredible improvisation named Luisa's trauma and brought her back from the edge of insanity and emotional breakdown.

Music's healing power comes especially after the truth of our pain and loss, whatever that may be, has been encountered face to face and perhaps even spoken out loud. Recently, Don took part in a worship service of healing at a mountain retreat center in North Carolina. Gathered there to pray and sing were large numbers of children and teens, together with an equal number of adults. At a designated time, the congregation was invited to move toward one of several places to have a brief prayer for healing and an anointing with fragrant oil. Don remembers:

> I was surprised to see so many of the younger ones come forward. Some of them said, "Can we pray for my grandparents who are very sick?" And they received the anointing, a gesture of blessing with words about the Holy Spirit working to strengthen and to heal. Then one ten- or eleven-year-old boy came to my station. When I asked him for whom and for what we should pray, he replied, "Can we pray for me? Sometimes I'm awfully mean to other kids." All the time the whole assembly was gently repeating a song from Taizé, "Come and fill our hearts with your peace. You alone, O Lord, are holy. Come and fill our hearts with your peace, alleluia!"

Was there ever a more apt, healing marriage of simple harmony, gracious words, and a luminous moment for truth? Don feels that he will always see that child's face and hear his voice when that chant is sung.

Sometimes music sets us on the path toward wholeness, as it may have done for this young boy. Music that invites us to be honest about pain and loss can open us up and set us on the way to healing, both as individuals and within larger communities of belonging. We end this chapter with a hymn by Brian Wren that exhibits just such honesty. In the wake of September 11, as many not only grieved loss but questioned God, Wren found these words, mixing lament and hope with utter frankness:

> When pain and terror strike by chance, with causes
>   unexplained,
> When God seems absent or asleep, and evil unre-
>   strained,
> We crave an all-controlling force, ready to rule and
>   warn,
> But find, far-shadowed by a cross, a child in weakness
>   born.
> How deep the Wisdom of our God, how weak, but
>   truly wise,
> To risk, to sacrifice, to die, and from the grave arise,
> To shred the shroud of death and fate, freeing our
>   hearts for good.
> We breathe the ample air of hope and take our chance
>   with God.

Chapter 8

SING JUSTICE, SING FREEDOM

———

The more the two of us talk about our lives in music, the more we find ourselves thinking about matters of freedom and justice. Singing about justice and freedom leads Emily directly to engaging in the struggle for justice. For Don music in worship must not only praise God, it must also offer a prophetic call to serve a suffering, needy world. In this chapter we explore ways in which music can sing about freedom and justice and also consider how singing itself can be an act of justice and freedom.

Many members of Don's generation remember the impact of a song from the 1960s, "If I Had a Hammer." Many groups recorded the song, but Pete Seeger's and Peter, Paul, and Mary's versions are the ones Don remembers most clearly. This popular song of protest played a part in the awakening of a sleepy 1950s generation to questions of injustice, connecting across age groups as support for the civil rights movement spread. It sang not only protest but also a vision of hope about "love between my brothers and my sisters all over this land." When Joan Baez sang it, her voice sounded like a bell of freedom.

Emily remembers growing up hearing this song at outdoor concerts, with the musicians jamming on stage. Little did we know at the time how deeply committed to social justice she, Amy, and many of their future musician friends would be. Many have come to admire the way in which the Indigo Girls and other popular musicians have supported a range of causes: Habitat for Humanity, environmental concerns, Native American education, and civil rights for minorities. And what Emily has done through her music, Don has done within the church, trying to help worshiping communities embrace their ethical responsibilities through hymns, sung prayer, and ritual song. Thus, the two of us find ourselves speaking to one another about justice across generations and across genres. We keep asking: How can our music address injustice, suffering, and oppression while also maintaining artistic quality? This is a question about music making, but it is also about the quality of our attention to the human situations about which we sing on stage or in the sanctuary.

YEARNING FOR JUSTICE, SINGING FOR FREEDOM

If you ever doubted the connection between singing and matters of human justice, just read any page or two of *Voices from the Mountains,* a book by Guy and Candie Carawan of the Highlander Folk Center in Tennessee, where many participants in the civil rights movement and other freedom struggles have received training and support since the 1930s. This book is a companion to their recordings of the songs of men and women from Appalachia from the 1940s through the early 1970s. Better yet, listen. This music comes out of struggle, pain, and courage in the face of economic hardships that are difficult for many of us to imagine today. These songs and the recollections about them are evidence of how music sustained resilience and survival, protest and affirmation. They are often also graced by a lively sense of humor. Take, for example, this recollection from Gurney Norman, whose family, like many others, had migrated north in search of work:

> That car of Daddy's was an old Pontiac he bought with the first wages he ever earned in Cincinnati. It had over a hundred thousand miles on it when he got it, but he never hesitated to take off in it for Kentucky. The first year we lived up there we never missed a week end going home. Fifty-two round trips in a year, over two hundred miles each way, six, seven, sometimes eight and nine people in it every run. Every Friday as soon as Daddy'd get home from work we'd load up and head out, and drive six straight hours south on old U.S. 25, through Lexington and Richmond, east into the hills on 421, then down state route 666 to the home place in Finley County.
>
> In the wintertime it would be dark before we even set out, but in the summers the light would hold 'til almost Richmond, and I remember the programs that came on the radio about that time

of day. My daddy played the guitar some, and he loved hillbilly music, and so at six o'clock he'd tune in the *Hillbilly Hit Parade* out of WCKY in Cincinnati. I remember it started and ended with somebody's fierce picking of the "Steel Guitar Rag," and then when it was over Wayne Rainey and Lonnie Glossen would come on, trying to sell harmonica instruction courses. Wayne and Lonnie were good musicians too, and when they'd get wound up Daddy would get excited and start to sing along with them, and bounce around in his seat and beat on the steering wheel with his hand. He'd cut up like that for miles and miles. He'd tickle us all so much we'd forget how uncomfortable we were, piled on top of one another in the back seat of that old car.

Many songs and stories were generated in protest against the harsh working conditions and the rape of the land that accompanied coal mining. "Dreadful mem'ries, how they linger," sang Sarah Ogan Gunning to the tune "Precious Memories": "How they ever flood my soul, How the workers and their children died from hunger and from cold." The song tells of management thugs, of violence, of oppressive work. As the wife and daughter of coal miners, Sarah saw much devastation, including her own child's death by starvation. No wonder the song cries out:

> Really, friends, it doesn't matter, whether you are black or white.
> The only way you'll every change things is to fight and fight and fight.

This song was not written for the concert hall or for the entertainment industry; and it was rarely, if ever, heard in church. Rather, this song is a cry from the earth and from the heart of a people who yearn to be free of economic and social oppression—a cry that also transforms that yearning into action on behalf of justice.

In 1981 Don met ninety-year-old ex-miner Nimrod Workman and heard him perform a number of his songs. Workman was particularly forceful about the scourge of black lung disease among the miners. Taking a traditional melody, often from a religious song, he would adapt its words into a cry for justice. For example, to the tune "Don't You Want to Go" he would sing:

> Don't you want to go with me to that land where I go?
> Be no strip mining in that land . . .
> No low wages in that land . . .
> No exploitation in that land . . .
> Be no black lung in that land . . .
> Be no politicians in that land . . .
> Be no sickness in that land . . .
> No Tony Boyle [an especially corrupt union leader] in
>   that land . . .
> Don't you want to go with me to that land?

The words are a plea for release from economic and social hardship, but the melody and plaintive harmony still carry the older evangelical religious fervor of this song that many before Workman had sung about heaven. Like many other effective songs of protest, Workman's new words were very specific, naming the new realities of suffering and oppression.

Whenever human beings are caught in oppressive suffering, songs emerge. Some of these songs voice pure lament, whereas others express the resiliency of humor and escape. Sometimes those who hear these songs in the public arena to which they are chiefly addressed forget or have never known that the songs—and also the call of freedom and the cries for justice they express—have roots in religious traditions. In the civil rights and anti-apartheid movements in the United States and in South Africa, these roots were often clear, as in the South African freedom song *"Siyahamba,"* whose refrain, "We are marching in the light of God," makes the body and the mind move. The first time the two of us sang *"Siyahamba"* was in a church gathering when Nelson Mandela was still in prison. It spoke to us immediately.

For Americans of every race, the most powerful examples of freedom's song come from the African American traditions of song and worship that emerged during the struggle up from slavery. We are convinced that the history of the United States cannot be adequately comprehended apart from knowledge of this music. It echoes through the years, still awaiting new generations of singers and hearers. Together with the music of Appalachia, it provides songlines that offer testimony to a human struggle for justice and racial equality that still continues.

GATHERING TO SING FOR FREEDOM

The remarkable Smithsonian Folkways recording *Sing for Freedom* tells the story of the civil rights movement through song. Listening to the CD, we marveled once again at the way hymns, spirituals, and gospel songs com-

A SONG TO SING, A LIFE TO LIVE

mingled with speeches and prayers to unify that profoundly important struggle. Our family lived through
those years in the inner city in New Haven, Connecticut,
where Don was studying and teaching at Yale and serving as musician to a church near our home in the predominantly African American Dixwell Avenue community.
Emily's early memories are of the housing project in
which we lived and of the urban grade school she attended. Our family was deeply committed to the movement.

Listening to the field recordings on *Sing for Freedom*
brings back the tension, the pain, the courage, and the
hope of those years. We recall the violence that overtook
our national life with the assassinations of the Kennedys,
of Dr. Martin Luther King Jr., of Medgar Evers, of civil
rights workers—the list is long. "Keep Your Hand on the
Plow" sang the perseverance that got those who were
working for freedom through their challenging days, days
that started when "I Woke Up This Morning with My
Mind Stayed on Freedom," as another song put it. "Ain't
Gonna Let Nobody Turn Me 'Round," the freedom
workers sang into the teeth of dogs and the watery as-
saults from fire hoses that were turned against them,
adapting the other verses to name those who were perse-
cuting them. When this traditional song was first adapted
by the movement in Albany, Georgia, the names of the
chief of police and the major were included: "Ain't gonna
let Chief Pritchett turn me 'round. . . . Ain't gonna let
Mayor Kelly turn me 'round." In this they used the same
pattern Nimrod Workman and others in the coal-mining
regions had used, steeling themselves for resistance to

specific people in specific places and writing in their verses the actual history of their protests.

One of the most significant gatherings of the civil rights movement took place in Atlanta in May 1964. The Sing for Freedom workshop, which was sponsored by the Highlander Folk School, the Southern Christian Leadership Conference, and the Student Nonviolent Coordinating Committee, brought together the musical protest traditions of the North and the South. Musicians and activists came from all over, listening and sharing songs from their own local communities. Present were powerful singers and songwriters who were part of the movement in the South, such as Fannie Lou Hamer, Bernice Reagon (later of Sweet Honey in the Rock), Cordell Reagon, and Betty May Fikes. From the North came well-known singers Phil Ochs, Tom Paxton, and Theodore Bikel.

Sing for Freedom may have looked and felt like a festival, but it was clearly also an event of great political importance to the civil rights struggle. As Guy and Candie Carawan told Don in an interview, "For some young freedom fighters, it was a revelation to hear some of the songs and history that had gone before." Imagine what it must have been to be with the Georgia Sea Island Singers; Doc Reese from the Texas prison system; Ed Young, the cane fife player from Mississippi; and the Moving Star Hall Singers from Johns Island, South Carolina. Fresh songs also emerged in this creative cauldron, as unexpected new verses were added to older melodies.

"The variety of styles was overwhelming," writes Joshua Dunson in his memoir of those four days, *Freedom in the Air.*

In the song "This Little Light of Mine," five, six, seven or eight leaders would introduce verses that were from their communities. Betty Mae Fikes of Selma, Alabama, whose voice is steel, set the pace with the clapping of her hands: "Up and I'm bleeding / I'm going to let it shine," singing despite the violence done to her. Doc Reese sang: "Voting for my freedom, I'm going to let it shine. Let it shine. Let it shine." There was that tremendous impact that only occurs when 50 or 60 song leaders bring their voices and clapping together in thunderbolts of song for 20, 25 minutes of letting your whole body explode into song.

Other older, quieter veterans also made contributions. Three women from a small town in South Carolina offered to sing songs their local communities had been singing for a long time:

> I feel like to go ahead
> Go ahead, go ahead
> Well, there's something tell me
> Go ahead.
> Sing a song, go ahead.

Dunson reports that a Reverend Aikens began to preach, and they began to sing:

> I'm marching to be all right (three times)
> Someday segregation will be over
> And I'll be free at last.
> I'm marching to be all right someday.

The newer freedom songs commingled with some of the Northern broadside songs from the union movement, such as "There once was a union maid, who never was afraid, of the goons and the geeks and the company sneaks." But then there were the older "Negro songs," like Doc Reese's chain gang rhythmic chants, and the Sea Island Singers dancing and singing old slave songs and stories that retained close ties to African forms. All this variety led to strong clashes of opinion. Many of the young people who had not heard the older songs found them distasteful; the younger black radicals did not want to hear songs that carried the memory of slaves or of the religion they had embraced in their oppression.

In those heated exchanges at the Atlanta gathering, some argued that those old songs were not just oppressive memories of a dark past. Rather, the old songs also carried a history of a people's hope for freedom. The very fact that this music had survived the Middle Passage— the forced journey across the sea from Africa—was a testimony to the power of African American people, they argued. Moreover, songs with religious meaning had been subverted, with their meaning hidden from owners through a kind of code. Thus, "Steal away, steal away, steal away to Jesus" referred not simply to wanting to be with Jesus by-and-by but also signaled that it was time to head to freedom by the Underground Railroad. By the end of those four days in 1964, a new fusion of the old and the new had begun to take place. Many of the younger members of the Student Nonviolent Coordinating Committee and the Southern Christian Leadership Conference acknowledged the connection between the old and new traditions of song. And the impact on some of the Northern songwriters and singers was unmistakable, as they came to realize that what had been preserved in the deep religious vision and cry for freedom in the Southern oral traditions was now the taproot of contemporary songs of protest and hope.

Although the beginnings of the civil rights movement are often associated with the 1955 Montgomery bus boycott, in fact, the movement had already begun in the deep memory of longing for freedom etched in the spirituals and in the gospel singing of the churches that were soon sending protesters to the picket lines. In all this music, lament and hope had been combined in energizing ways. This kind of energy still exists wherever such music is sung, as those who recognized the name of Bernice Johnson Reagon in the account of the 1964 gathering will know. During the 1960s she and Cordell Reagon, Rutha Harris, and Charles Heblett were known as the Student Nonviolent Coordinating Committee Freedom Singers. Today the unmistakable quality of her voice and the musical genius of the a cappella singing they employed can still be heard in the energizing music of Sweet Honey in the Rock.

HYMNS THAT CARRY A SOCIAL VISION

The power of song in stirring up longing and hope for social justice can also work on other communities. Few people—including many churchgoers—are aware that the hymnals of the majority-white churches also incorporate powerful texts that articulate the Christian calling to work for freedom and justice. One that we have both recently sung in worship is "The Voice of God Is Calling." The text, set to a sturdy tune, sets these words in God's mouth: "I hear my people crying in cot and mine and slum." And it asks of the singers, "Who will go to help my people in need?"

As we searched our hymnals for texts that carry the message of justice, we were both surprised at how many carry the message of social justice yet also by how thoroughly most have been neglected. "O God of Earth and Altar" cries out to God about how "earthly powers falter" as "people drift and die." Some hymns incorporate words directly from the biblical prophets, such as "What Does the Lord Require?" with its line "Do justice, love mercy, walk humbly with your God." Sometimes the words echo New Testament visions of hope, as in "O Holy City Seen of God," which calls those who sing to build a fair and just society.

A recent example comes from Brian Wren, who takes his cue from a vision of the prophet Isaiah:

> Arise, shine out, your light has come, unfolding city of
>   our dreams.
> On distant hills a glory gleams: the new creation has
>   begun.
> Above earth's valleys, thick with night, high on your
>   walls the dawn appears,
> and history shall dry its tears, as nations march toward
>   your light.

The text speaks of the sounds of violence ceasing and finally sings the full vision of a restored, renewed earth:

> The dancing air shall glow with light, and sun and
>   moon give up their place,
> when love shines out of every face, our good, our glory,
>   and delight.

Emily and Don have heard this sung by an assembly that tries to live in this light, with love shining out of every face. Though it belongs to the Christian tradition, it echoes a universal yearning, especially in the present world where too much violence exists and too many tears fall. In a time when the nations desperately need it, this ancient text still sings with hope.

From folk traditions in Scotland comes another new song, John Bell's "The Summons." Set to a lilting melody, it calls the singers into ever deepening ways of justice and mercy. Recently, we heard this sung boldly by a congregation accompanied by tin whistle and guitar. The music keeps asking in Christ's voice: "Will you follow me if I but call your name?" showing that those who respond will "care for cruel and kind" and "set the prisoners free and never be the same." It asks the singing assembly: "Will you use the faith you've found to reshape the world around?" The summons is to a new kind of spirituality in following the God who is already about the work of mercy and healing and justice in the world. "Now that's a religion I respond to," we overheard someone say after our community sang this song together.

"Why don't we sing more songs like this at church?" Emily has challenged Don.

"I too wonder about this," he replied. "Part of the answer is that the music of these hymns is often difficult or out of current popularity. The tunes and the texts both make demands of worshipers that are not always user-friendly. I also wonder if some of these hymns and songs are simply too uncomfortable for many people. When music and words push us beyond our comfort zones on matters of social ethics and our larger societal responsibilities, many of us begin to squirm. Perhaps some also worry that singing these would violate appropriate boundaries between religious faith and politics."

We suspect that others may be worried about how making the commitment to justice that the songs ask would change their lives. Hymns that sing of justice and freedom ought to agitate and disturb many of us. Such songs can bring us face-to-face with truths we might rather not know. However, when the church does not learn to sing these challenging songs of faith, it may find that the impulse to justice and freedom is heard only outside its walls.

Many popular groups appeal to those alienated from organized religion precisely by embracing the subversive potential of music. So Public Enemy's song "Don't Believe the Hype" sings something that church and synagogue should take to heart. We do not mean that religious communities should sing that particular lyric in worship. However, we are both convinced that people of religious faith do have a stake in singing about justice and hope for the human family and also that authentic religious traditions have much to offer to the world on this point. In times of great suffering and under massive systems of so-

A Song to Sing, A Life to Live

cial deception, people of faith need to risk singing on the subversive side of struggle—just as those who sang in earlier movements for justice did. Without religious faith many of the world's struggles for justice would not have happened.

Some of the most interesting recent hymns contain appropriate self-criticism on these matters from within the Christian community. When a church sang Fred Pratt Green's hymn "When the Church of Jesus Shuts Its Outer Door" for the first time not long ago, several members of the congregation mentioned that the hymn startled them in a good way: "That hymn was as powerful as the sermon."

Perhaps the most promising new strands in many churches' singing come from global music sources. These are hymns and songs from Africa, the Pacific Rim, and Latin America. *"Cuando el Pobre,"* which we mentioned in Chapter Five, is printed in both English and Spanish in several contemporary hymnals. The song is liberation theology set to music: it invites an English-speaking congregation to cross over into another language and culture while affirming that God identifies first of all with those who are poor.

Hymns and songs that call for the transformation of communities and society as a whole are available to the church, and more are emerging each year. This music can teach first-world Christians to sing the truth about their own complicity in injustice. Faith requires more than singing only what we already know. It is too easy to hear only what sustains the old pieties and behaviors. Our experience both inside and outside the churches urges us to look for songs that call us to new action, new attitudes, and an active solidarity with the suffering of this world. And that requires honest self-awareness and the strength that comes from being rooted in God's own freedom and justice.

MUSICIANS AND MUSIC
THAT MAKE A DIFFERENCE

Emily and Amy count it a great privilege to have performed and traveled with Joan Baez. She once told Emily about some of her performances in Eastern Europe during the years of Communist rule. She spoke of how governmental authorities threatened to shut down her concerts because they feared that the vision of social justice in her songs would stimulate political protest. These rulers knew that songs can give courage to human beings who are living under oppression. Songs such as *"Siyahamba"* (We are marching in the light of God) played a significant role during the anti-apartheid movement in South Africa.

The music of freedom can change people, freeing them from prejudices even when not explicitly linked to protest. An acquaintance of ours confessed that he had had a negative attitude toward all Cubans under the Castro regime until he began to listen to the music of the Buena Vista Social Club. "If people can sing like that, I can't let my political ideas belittle their humanity," he later confessed. Music like this can be subversive just because it comes in under the radar—if it can get a hearing at all.

Emily and Amy are increasingly aware of how difficult it is to get certain music played on radio because of the ownership of so many stations by a few large media conglomerates. Yet new music that carries a vision of hope often gets known by word of mouth, bypassing the music industry's process of commercialization and cliché.

For Emily and many other musicians, playing benefit concerts provides an important way of being personally involved in supporting movements for justice and freedom. "We have been active in raising money and political awareness for environmental causes," Emily said of her involvement in several Honor the Earth tours.

> Both Amy and I have been deeply impressed with the views of many Native Americans about the land. For them it is a spiritual issue when indiscriminate development and big economic interests exploit the natural resources of the earth. So we have played benefit concerts to raise money for environmental education. One of the real joys of our musical efforts comes in meeting Native American activists, both on the reservations and elsewhere. Our music becomes an instrument of solidarity with so many who are struggling for land rights, energy justice, and for better conditions for their children and future generations. In the process Amy and I have come to respect their lives and spiritual traditions. We try to be bridges between people who respond to our songs and the need for awareness and action.

The Indigo Girls' work for social causes has inspired Don to increase his own attempts to awaken church musicians to their responsibility for the prophetic side of the church's song.

One of Emily's most vivid experiences in music making occurred at the 1993 march on Washington in support of gay and lesbian rights.

> It was at the Mall in D.C. There were hundreds of thousands of people there and a huge stage. We thought about the other great gatherings, especially the 1963 march on Washington when Martin Luther King Jr. proclaimed his "I Have a Dream" speech amidst a great deal of singing. We were nervous, I remember, walking up those rickety scaffolding stairs to the huge stage in front of the vast audience. We sang, voices alone, Paul Simon's "American Tune." Suddenly, everybody was with us and we with them. The music created solidarity and a sense of power for people who had been typically discounted and oppressed by so much prejudice.

Music has taken Emily and Amy to many places:

> to the Berlin Wall as it was falling, playing while it was literally being chipped away with hammers. We went to Chiapas, to stand in solidarity with the Zapatistas and indigenous peoples, simply trying to live without economic exploitation and military violence. More recently, I went to Vieques with friends, one of whom was from Puerto Rico. At that time, the U.S. Navy was still using the island for bombing practice. We took part in one of the protest camps. When I got there, I was scared. No one could assure us that

A SONG TO SING, A LIFE TO LIVE

we were safe, especially since someone had been accidentally killed recently in a bombing test. The military guards were laughing and joking at our little group. We gathered in a circle and sang with my friend Lourdes in Spanish words to the effect that "I have life in my hands." I sang "Everything in Its Own Time," an antiwar song about grace and patience for good things to come back around again. I didn't realize the significance of the group's witness until, on the way back in the boat, Lourdes broke out into song again: "Where are you going my friend? I'm going to Vieques to get the Navy out." Others began tapping on metal parts of the boat until everyone was singing and making rhythm with hands and feet. Like our experience in Chiapas, I know that in times of great struggle, turmoil, and political resistance, music is a powerful force for unity.

Both of us admire those musicians who have engaged in great struggles. Most of the people who are moved by songs of freedom are not professional musicians, but at certain times great artists in every genre of music and song come together with ordinary people to express the deepest human longing for freedom and a more just world. Humble musical art and great musical art both have the power, at the right time, to inspire new vision and new hope.

Don enjoyed an association with the late Robert Shaw, one of the world's foremost choral conductors. Shaw's career with the Robert Shaw Chorale and later with the Atlanta Symphony Orchestra and Chorus is legendary. In 1988 the symphony and chorus toured behind the Iron Curtain in East Berlin. Their program included Beethoven's Ninth Symphony. An orchestra player described how, as the triumphant notes concluded the ecstatic final movement, Maestro Shaw raised a clenched fist on high. After a moment's silence, the audience rose to its feet and erupted in thunderous applause. That performance was a musical witness against years of an oppressive political regime. Beethoven's great symphony proclaims Schiller's text about joy, freedom, and brotherhood; and on that night, this text was heard as a cry for freedom. The Berlin Wall was to fall within a few months. Now every time his congregation sings the hymn "Joyful, Joyful, We Adore Thee" to that theme from the Ninth Symphony, Don hears an echo of that inspiring night in East Berlin.

If one of our most important human responsibilities is speaking truth to power when power is corrupt, we can be grateful when history gives us music that sings truth to power. Music has been and still remains an instrument of social vision and change. At its deepest root is a powerful religious and spiritual impulse.

At the same time, both sacred and secular music can ignore and even subvert the cry for freedom and justice. How the music of explicitly religious traditions and so-called secular music clash or converge is where our conversation now turns.

Chapter 9

SATURDAY NIGHT AND SUNDAY MORNING

———

W hat do Aretha Franklin and Sylvia McNair have in common? Ask a fan of black gospel music or an opera music critic and the answer might be "Very little." Both are singers, but there is also something else, something more than meets the ear. Both of them are musical crossovers in ways that interest both Emily and Don. Aretha Franklin's singing began in church and moved out to be a dominant presence in popular music. Her voice was formed in hearing the preaching of her famous father, the Reverend C. L. Franklin, and her voice still works in church as well as on recordings. Sylvia McNair has an exquisite classically trained voice, but she also can sing jazz well. She is one of a number of operatic singers who cross over from the recital hall to the recording studio. These women show that some of our categories and standard ways of thinking about music and musicians—religious, secular, classical, popular, sacred—are too narrow.

In writing this book, it has often seemed to us that we represent two halves of a musical equation: Emily the secular and the popular, Don the sacred and the church. But we have concluded that the line between church and nonchurch cannot be drawn as sharply as many people—including us—think. Both of us found ourselves working along the boundaries between church and nonchurch, between the realm of the sacred and what is considered secular. Music in its various and varied forms has taken us to very different venues and shaped us in different ways, to be sure; but some of Emily's strong influences have come from her religious roots, and some of Don's have come out of jazz, spirituals, and blues. We have come to think of our conversations and our musical lives as Saturday night (Emily) and Sunday morning (Don)—and to see that these songlines are always crossing back and forth into territory that is new.

Sometimes it seems that people who think of themselves as exclusively interested in either religious music or secular music like to compare the best that their side possesses with the worst of the other. So we should begin by admitting that both can be done badly. Religious music can shut off reality, and secular music, especially in its more commercial forms, can substitute manipulation for mystery and insight. Sometimes a religious community sings what is eternally true, sometimes nothing but self-congratulations. Sometimes popular music deals out nothing but banality; sometimes it strikes at the heart of our hopes and fears. There are many surprises both inside and outside the church. Saturday night and Sunday morning are always in an ongoing conversation, sometimes quarreling, sometimes in mutual respect. The cliché is that they are somehow incompatible.

As you may recall, the story of our musical lives begins with Emily's grandfather and Don's father, Harold. Hal (as he was usually known) was a man who was a Saturday night *and* Sunday morning guy. We have pictures of him at the Astor Hotel in New York, a twenty-something jazzman. He played sax, clarinet, and violin and also sang in the 1920s and early 1930s; that's just what the frontline players did. He played with some of the most respected bands of the time: Russ Morgan, Paul Specht, Harl Smith, Jack Teagarden, and even on a short recording stint with Paul Whiteman.

But Hal was a musician for Sunday morning as well. Sometime just after World War II, a Methodist preacher decided that he would like to form a Sunday school orchestra to play hymns and little arrangements before the church service began during what was then called the Sunday school assembly. He insisted that Hal Saliers would be just the person to organize and lead it. Taking on that responsibility somehow began to change Hal's own self-image from that of a musically gifted drunk to that of a musically gifted Sunday morning fixture. Saturday night music had almost taken Hal away from his family, but Sunday morning music gave Don his father back. To this day Don can picture Hal's lead violin waving to give tempo and direction to Don and the other players. That communal playing and singing was a surprising gift to the church, to the son, and to the father.

Crossing Over and Back

In a recent National Public Radio interview, Dave Brubeck, the great jazz musician now in his eighties, talked about the influence of Johann Sebastian Bach on his music. He spoke of how the same melody used in a folk tune or even a drinking song would show up in a sacred piece of music, though its meaning would always be changed by new harmonies and tempos. Brubeck himself is a skilled performer and composer in both jazz and classical styles. A recent recording, *Classical Brubeck,* is a collaboration between the London Symphony Orchestra, a large oratorio chorus, and his own quartet. Don has vivid memories of hearing this famous quartet with Paul Desmond on sax at Basin Street East in New York many years ago. The fugues and intimate dialogue between sax, piano, bass, and drums were simply permeated with classical elements. And yet these players could swing with the best. The experiments with different time signatures led to the breakthrough *Take Five* album, in which 5/4 time suddenly became part of jazz ever after. Of course, Brubeck knew that classical music had used 5/4 and many other usual rhythmic patterns well before; among his teachers and influences was French composer Darius Milhaud.

One of the things that makes Brubeck such an important figure is his own deep religious faith. This comes through in his sacred music, beginning with the oratorio "Light in the Wilderness." Early struggles against racism while in the military, his enormous joy in life expressed through jazz, and his profound respect for the mystery of

God all bear fruit in the work of this great musician. Brubeck came recently to Emory University to give a master class and perform. The enthusiastic intergenerational response to him was evidence of the power of music. Students were buzzing about his range and his obvious great humanity. He is a true crossover soul. Can you imagine how delighted we were when Matt Brubeck, a fine cellist who is Dave's son, toured with Amy and Emily one season? The crossing over continues into the next generation.

The first time Don heard Emily and Amy perform "Hammer and a Nail," he recognized a phrase of an old hymn, "Let Us Break Bread Together," played in a simple guitar line as the words of the song die away. The words of that phrase come straight from the church background of their growing up: "When I fall on my knees with my face to the rising sun, O Lord, have mercy on me." Don asked Emily whether she had intentionally included this phrase. "Of course," she said, "the whole song sings about getting up and building something together. It's a call to work for others, and one shouldn't do this presumptively. We all need mercy." *Exactly so,* Don thought; hearing the echo of a church song about a common holy meal that asks for mercy is right on target. Here is a song that could well be the motto of Habitat for Humanity, but how many of us who sing this in church actually make that connection between faith at work and the need for mercy?

The more we have explored this idea of crossing over between what we think are quite separate realms of music, the more we have realized that this is often how music changes. There have always been borrowings from one realm to another. As early as the 1940s, some black gospel singers were moving in some of the new directions that would later contribute to rock 'n' roll. Elvis Presley, so influenced by church and black musical traditions while growing up in Memphis, recorded both gospel songs and his hip-swinging "Hound Dog." He knew the contrast and the affinities between Saturday night and Sunday morning. Aretha Franklin, the preacher's daughter, does too. In her performances we hear the distinctive black church style of singing, which she often brings directly over into her popular recordings and soul performances. More recently, singers such as Amy Grant, who was a major popular Christian artist, crossed over into love songs that no longer focused on God but rather on human relationships. Meanwhile, Christian popular music has grown into a multimillion dollar industry that draws on a range of popular styles, from rap and hip-hop to heavy metal and easy listening, all fitted out with specifically Christian lyrics. And great operatic and concert vocal performers such as Renee Fleming and Bryn Terfel have recorded hit albums that take them into the domain of pop and jazz styles.

The great cellist Yo-Yo Ma has moved through an enormous range of music, crossing the lines between the recognized classical works to the popular music of various cultures, most recently of Brazil. Several of our friends practically weep over *Yo-Yo Ma, Soul of the Tango,* his recording of tango music composed by Astor Piazzolla.

Many church hymns and choral pieces began as music outside the church. There is a long history of putting sacred texts to popular nonchurch melodies in order to speak to a wider audience. A good example of this is the tune for the Holy Week hymn "O Sacred Head Now Wounded." Its original words were a love song— "Confused are all my feelings. A tender maid's the cause"—set to a medieval melody by Hans Leo Hassler in 1601. Not exactly a theological text! Millions of Christians sing this hymn about the passion of Christ, harmonized by Bach and known as the "Passion Chorale," unaware of the tune's origin. The religious words, which originated in the twelfth century, were first set to this tune in 1656 by the German composer Johann Crueger.

Classical musicians who do not consider themselves religious often speak of performing great works such as Handel's *Messiah* or Bach's Mass in B Minor as great spiritual experiences. In these works words that are usually spoken in worship are embraced within the context of the concert hall. Perhaps the spirituality these musicians encounter there is close to what many young adults mean when they say, "I'm not very religious, but I am spiritual." Although organized religion may be suspect for them, the musical and artistic expressions of faith still hold great meaning.

We have been in some places that convince us that it is possible to find more church in the music outside church buildings than inside. Emily speaks with great affection of the "ragtag crowds in the late 1980s in Atlanta at the Little Five Points Pub." She and Amy began to play regular gigs there and developed friendships with other aspiring musicians. The people who came to listen were of a very diverse character—from college kids, many from dysfunctional families, to kids on the edge of poverty who were living on the streets. A lot of broken lives seemed to be held together by the music making in that place. Emily remembers having "long talks about the real issues of life, as folks sought comfort and consolation. Then we would jam and create a space for real joy!" Now that strikes us both as a pretty good description of what a church might be.

However, the church at its best may sing of realities that a completely secularized sensibility might too easily dismiss or reject. When a thousand voices sing "For All the Saints, Who from Their Labors Rest" to honor a life well lived, something splendid is at work in the "blest communion, fellowship divine" that links those who sing with those who have died. When the simple elegance of the Dutch tune "What Is This Place" is sung by a large Mennonite congregation in strong four parts without accompaniment, an image and experience of community that the world sorely needs emerges as the singers describe the church as "only a house" but realize that it also becomes "a body that lives when we are gathered here and know that God is near." Such hymns lead the two of us to think that the church may even have language the world needs if it is to understand itself more fully.

PROFANING THE SACRED, BLESSING THE PROFANE

The church has a long history of resistance to nonsacred musical styles and instruments. Beginning in the Middle

Ages, the Roman Catholic tradition favored plainsong as the most acceptable style of music for use in public worship. Debate about expanding this preference to include other forms raged throughout the twentieth century, evoking a series of official documents on sacred music. The first, published in 1903 under Pope Pius X, declared that Gregorian chant was the proper music of liturgy and drew a sharp line between worship music and secular music, especially the music that might appear in theaters and other popular venues. Classical polyphony was allowed, but art music and instruments such as piano and saxophone were prohibited. Not until the 1950s did the Vatican recognize hymns sung in languages other than Latin. After the Second Vatican Council (1962–1965), musical change accelerated, especially with the advent of the folk Mass that emerged later in the 1960s. Although official documents retain the old distinction between sacred and secular music, in practice Roman Catholic church music is now influenced by an incredible variety of sources that the official documents never envisioned, except in the negative. But of course, there are always gains and losses. Some long for the solemn mystery of the Latin Mass, while others come alive to worship with indigenous African American settings.

Protestants have also been suspicious of certain music and have invoked a strong distinction between sacred and secular. In some Protestant circles, the violin played as a fiddle raises eyebrows; some have called the fiddle the devil's box because they associate it with dancing and loose social life. But that too is changing as Appalachian folk styles are being recovered. Once at a fiddling contest in Vermont, we sat on blankets under the stars and heard players from Nova Scotia, Maine, and other northeastern states. Someone nearby said that one lone player from Asheville, North Carolina, "played the devil out of the fiddle."

The so-called worship wars, which we explored in Chapter Six, can be understood in part as struggles about what is holy and what is not, about what is sacred and what is secular. Some of the crossing over that has provoked these "wars" has been introduced as an effort to reach people outside organized religion, who don't know the older hymns, and who, some fear, might find their structured form and rich language incomprehensible, as if these were part of some kind of secret code known only to churchgoers. So in the name of outreach, some congregations have developed a praise band that plays forms of rock music fitted with simple Christian lyrics—a new combination of what is supposedly secular with the sacred.

It should be clear by now that we see nothing wrong with such crossing over in itself. Yet in each case, the question remains whether every style is equally suitable for worship. We are grieved when hasty answers to this question lead to animosity within the church, when the partisans of praise bands and the advocates of organs dismiss one another and refuse to listen—something that happens on both sides of the conflict.

Yet finally, some nonjudgmental judgments are necessary, because every congregation cannot and should not mush every musical style together in every worship service. As the church continues to struggle along this crossover border, we hope that congregations can hold on to the poetry and language and music that has stood the test of time—yet without closing off the emerging poetry and music that may become part of the larger tradition years from now. And we hope that those who favor new forms will not take the easy path of rejecting the more demanding words and music of the greater religious tradition whenever a newer popular style appears. The Anglican dean William Inge is reported to have said that the church that marries the spirit of the age may be a widow in the next generation. With care and attention over time, a local community can begin to sense that some music does touch deeper realities than other music can. When this happens, the community can recognize some very accessible and popular music as not worth holding on to for long, not because it is bad but rather because it soon needs replacing with newer, more immediately accessible music.

This is what the two of us look for and long for: music that offers something to grow into, that isn't soon exhausted, and that does not replicate in simple clichés whatever is popular at the moment. Though we often differ in particular judgments, we both believe that crossovers between different kinds of music can be a source of richness when one keeps this standard in mind.

One way for religious communities to explore the boundaries of musical change is to realize that they need not restrict all their music making to times of worship. Many churches have successful coffeehouse evenings, and still other churches and synagogues sponsor a range of concerts and musical events. Sponsoring and collaborating in making music available to the neighborhood or larger urban community provides a space within which to engage popular styles and also time to ponder whether they fit in worship. Beyond this, religious communities should actually listen to and share the messages, the images, the emotional content of music generated in the more general culture. As we have both tried to say in these pages, the sounds of pain and suffering, joy and courage, outrage and silence are present in both popular and classical music. Increasingly, we are also hearing the way people actually struggle with and celebrate life in global music. As we have noted throughout this book, new and traditional songs from African, Latin and South American, Pacific Rim, and South Asian sources are finding their way into new hymnals and songbooks, also influencing popular and classical music.

At the same time, we want to insist that the church also has something to say to the world from out of its own treasures, including traditional hymnody as well as emerging forms. Chant still speaks to a new generation. A few years ago, a CD of chant from a group of Spanish monks was something of a surprise popular hit. The worship music style of the French community of Taizé has made a remarkable impact on unchurched seekers. It is basically a modified form of chant, with classical harmonic patterns. Recently, someone said in our hearing, "These short pieces are like meditative praise choruses, only more like prayer." A flood of new hymns are being written by poets who share the realism and honesty of the best of other songwriters who operate outside churches and synagogues. One of these is Brian Wren, whose text we included at the end of Chapter Seven.

Don often works with religious communities to help them think about music for worship. In these contexts he reports,

> The first thing I often say is that music can evoke the divine and not necessarily mention God all the time. Not all music with religious import needs to be explicitly liturgical, that is, addressed to God. Of course, in worship the assembly prays and sings to God. At the same time, any music that explores human life in all its range of extremity and ordinariness can evoke the presence (or the absence) of God. Music that moves toward the good, the true, the just, and the beautiful often brings a sense of transcendence to hearers. The plain fact is that the church can often hide from God simply by uttering the words of unreflective piety. The appearance of religious words is no guarantee of authentic praise. Some nonchurch music that truly expresses the heart's torment, the soul's lament, or the ecstatic joy we experience within the beauty of creation may be more religious than hymns with poor theology sung without conviction.

For both of us, playing along the border of Saturday night and Sunday morning calls us back again and again to seeing how important it is that neither side let stereotypes and clichés determine its music. If we have learned anything from one another and from where music has taken us thus far in our lives, it is this: listen attentively to music before making quick judgments, especially negative ones. Let the richness of the music and the quality of each performance influence your listening and your conversations. And look for the places at which both professedly religious people and those searching outside the boundaries of organized religion do in fact hear something in common that presses beyond the obvious. There are places when people do come together to experience how music calls out mystery and a vision of life beyond their managed truisms. This may occur in great cathedral spaces, such as St. John the Divine in New York during winter solstice, or in the streets as a protest song redirects the listeners' political and social energies. Such convergence may occur when a litany of the names of the dead are sung in a liturgical event or at a public remembrance of September 11. On such occasions factions dissolve, and people of every persuasion can be renewed.

When all is said and done, a lot is at stake in the dialogue between Saturday night and Sunday morning. On both sides of this border, which really is not such a high one after all, those who love music will always encounter the great temptation of settling for music that asks nothing of us, music we enjoy only because it is familiar, music that does not press beyond categories to explore the beauty and the mystery of life. Whether for entertainment or for worship, excellence matters; and delight can come in surprising places.

As musicians of Saturday night and Sunday morning, the two of us especially want to encourage music that puts listeners in touch with the sources of human truth and flourishing. There is something profoundly spiritual about true musical artistry wherever it appears, especially when it is brought to music that takes us beyond our self-created images of ourselves and one another. The world needs music making, listening, and sharing such as this. Different kinds of music will bring us different experiences of delight and be appropriate to different situations in life. We may still say of particular songs or pieces of music, "That's sacred" and "That's secular." Musical tensions will continue to exist, but if we embrace them with an open spirit, they can carry us into explorations that are worthy of human beings who are truly alive, mortal, and searching.

Chapter 10

MUSIC AND THE SEARCH FOR GOD

———

The songlines we have traced in this book began with our own stories, but they have led us on a journey through the shared human territory of embodiment and identity, grieving and community, justice and joy. We have explored some of the wondrous places to which music has carried the two of us, and we hope we have helped you to recall some of the special places to which your own journey with music has taken you. Now we want to take one more step into the inexhaustible depth of music as a spiritual practice. We want to consider the songlines of human life as pathways along which we human beings find ourselves searching for God.

Even those who disavow specific religious beliefs or who choose to distance themselves from particular traditions may recognize that music engages the human spirit in a profound way. Its close relationship to feeling and emotion, its constant sounding of the elemental rhythms of life, its importance to personal and communal identity—all of these help us to glimpse the possibility that music is very much part of who we are at the most basic level. Yet music is also, at the very same time, a reality that comes from beyond ourselves. Drawing on the wisdom of religious traditions, we might name this possibility by saying that music is a means of communion between the human and the divine. Perhaps singing is humankind's most vital and most widely shared spiritual act because it awakens in us a shared solidarity and a resonance with the transcendent.

Abraham Joshua Heschel, the great twentieth-century Jewish thinker, described our human resonance with the transcendent as "the sense of the ineffable" and argued that this sense is "the root of [human] creative activities in art, thought and noble living." Expressing our sense of the ineffable, we "attempt to convey what we see and cannot say." This, says Heschel, "is the everlasting theme of [humankind's] unfinished symphony." His book *Man's Quest for God* is a wise and powerful exploration of the human search for the divine, an ongoing search in which many of today's spiritual seekers are engaged. Heschel especially urged cantors, who lead Jewish worshipers in song, not to be satisfied with what is too readily accessible but rather to press on toward mystery. "Religious music is an attempt to convey that which is within our reach but beyond our grasp," he noted. "The loss of that tension throws all cantorial music into the danger of becoming a distortion of the spirit." Again and again Heschel encourages his readers to be alert, to notice, to wonder, to be radically amazed: "to pray is to take notice

A SONG TO SING, A LIFE TO LIVE

of the wonder, to regain a sense of the mystery that animates all beings."

Heschel's wisdom about the mystery that animates all
life, including our lives as human beings, helps explain why
music is such an important part of our search for God.
Music thrives in the space created by the tension between
what we can imagine and what we can put into words, in
the vibrant space of possibility that exists in the gap between
our longings and our present reality. Living in this gap can
be painful at times; but if we inhabit it with openness and
wonder, it can be a place of amazement. In this space we are
embraced in all our restlessness. To be attentive and open to
wonder can also give us hope that in good time the tension
between now and someday—the distance between our
reach and our grasp—will ultimately be resolved.

Music Calls to the
Restless Heart

"Our hearts are restless until they find their rest in Thee,"
wrote the fifth-century Christian theologian Augustine of
Hippo in the first line of his autobiographical reflections
on his search for God, *Confessions*. The sense that the
human heart is restless also appears in a thousand ways in
popular song and is echoed in folk music, tribal song, and
Western classical music traditions. Human beings are
restless for many things—for love, security, a good harvest, a reason for being, home—and music has found
countless ways to express this restlessness. But note that

Augustine adds one more dimension to his understanding of human restlessness. That ending phrase, "in Thee," suggests that no limited thing can ever completely satisfy our restlessness. Instead, our restlessness draws us ever toward reality beyond the obvious, beyond the literal world of "what you see is what you get." It draws us toward God. And so although the first words in this ancient sentence state the obvious, the sentence as a whole speaks of a great mystery. "Our hearts are restless until they find their rest in Thee" is not just a statement; it is a prayer of acknowledgment and hope that human life will finally come to rest in the One who is both its first source and its ultimate fulfillment.

Anne Lamott, a writer who lives in Northern California, has also written autobiographically about the search for God. In her book *Traveling Mercies,* she tells of her intensely restless years of struggle as a young person and of her subsequent discovery of a true home in a small Christian church. Finding this church did not in any way diminish her lifelong lover's quarrel with all things orthodox, but it did bring her much healing. A key turning point takes place as she visits a flea market near Sausalito, California.

> If I happened to be there between eleven and one on Sundays, I could hear gospel music coming from a church right across the street. It was called St. Andrew Presbyterian, and it looked homely and impoverished, a ramshackle building with a cross on top, sitting on a small parcel of land with a few skinny pine trees. But the music wafting out was so pretty that I would stop and listen. I knew

a lot of the hymns from the times I'd gone to church with my grandparents and from the albums we'd had of spirituals. Finally, I began stopping in at St. Andrew from time to time, standing in the doorway to listen to the songs. I couldn't believe how run-down it was, with terrible linoleum that was brown and over shined, and plastic stained-glass windows. But it had a choir of five black women and one rather Amish-looking man making all that glorious noise, and a congregation of thirty people or so, radiating kindness and warmth. During the time when people hugged and greeted each other, various people would come back to where I stood to shake my hand or try to hug me; I was as frozen and stiff as Richard Nixon. After this, Scripture was read, and then the minister . . . would preach . . . and it would be . . . enough to send me running back to the sanctuary of the flea market. . . .

I went back to St. Andrew about once a month. No one tried to con me into sitting down or staying. I always left before the sermon. I loved singing, even about Jesus, but I just didn't want to be preached at about him. . . . Something inside me that was stiff and rotting would feel soft and tender. Somehow the singing wore down all the boundaries and distinctions that kept me so isolated. Sitting there, standing with them to sing, sometimes so shaky and sick that I felt like I might tip over, I felt bigger than myself, like I was being taken care of, tricked into coming back to life.

Not every person of restless heart just happens to be standing right outside a singing church. And to be honest, the singing that happens in some churches might not have lured Lamott in to listen. But something in Lamott resonated with this particular singing. What drew her to those human voices raised in praise and blessing also resonates with both of us. This kind of singing is a balm that soothed someone who felt sick and shaky and stiff. This singing reached in to embrace someone who felt isolated and to enlarge someone who felt vulnerable. This singing helped this listener to come back to life. We too have known communities of song in the midst of struggle and of joy who have sung their lives to God, and such song was itself life-giving.

How does God call us back to life through music? The two of us have asked one another this question many times while writing this book. We think that Anne Lamott's powerful Sunday morning experience provides one example of how sung faith can lead to healing and wholeness. Those of us who have spent lots of time inside the church sometimes have similar experiences. Beyond this, God-haunted music and song outside the church and the synagogue can also call to the restless heart, as we have seen at many points in this book.

Listening to music can be "a shattering experience, throwing the soul into an encounter with an aspect of reality to which the mind can never relate itself adequately," writes Rabbi Heschel. To some, like Lamott, the shattering experience loosens up the stiffness that has settled into the bones and prepares the way for healing. For others, Heschel suggests, music dislodges arrogance and induces a sense of contrition and a readiness for repentance. What is clear is this: whenever music touches us deeply, the potential for transformation exists. What we think and what we perceive about the world and about ourselves can change.

What music calls to your restless heart? Where in music does your soul encounter an aspect of reality that shatters your complacency or your fear?

One of Emily's favorite Christmas carols is "In the Bleak Midwinter." The early stanzas imagine the birth of Jesus in a stable where "frosty wind made moan" and the earth was "hard as iron, water like a stone." In the bleakness of this place, angels "may" have gathered, but the greatest gift came from the child's mother, who "worshiped the beloved with a kiss." After drawing the singers into this intimate scene, the final stanza poses a burning question: "What shall I give him, poor as I am?" And then it puts an answer on their lips: "What I can I give him? Give my heart." In the end, singing this carol, we are able to offer our very hearts but only because first this little one has come into our world. In this carol we acknowledge our poverty as mortal beings, "poor as I am," and we are empowered to make a fitting response to the mystery of God's own gift of life to the world.

Sometimes when the two of us have listened together to Bach's Mass in B Minor or to bagpipes playing "Amazing Grace" at a friend's funeral, we have glimpsed one more fundamental dynamic in how music opens the restless heart to respond to God. In musical moments like these, we understand that even while we are searching for God, God is also searching for us. In our experience this is a basic paradox of faith and of life: we do not find God through our searching; but rather in our searching, we come to understand that God is searching for us, desiring

175

to be with us and to know us fully. Charles Wesley, one of the greatest hymn writers in the English language, helps us to sing of this experience in the hymn "Love Divine, All Loves Excelling" as one of "love divine, all loves excelling, joy of heaven to earth come down." And the last line of this marvelous hymn leads us one more step into the land of paradox. When God finds us, Wesley has us sing, we are once again "lost" but in a most unexpected way, "lost in wonder, love and praise."

Whatever your religious convictions and whatever your quarrels or doubts with a specific tradition, know this: music, when brought to the service of ultimate things, can be a revelation. This is what all teachers of wisdom keep trying to tell us and what the most authentic strands of religious tradition keep before us. The whole creation does not belong to us; rather, it is given as gift, and music is the sound of this divine giving. When music finds us and claims all that we are, even if only from time to time, we are *found* in a very remarkable way. It is as though we ourselves were re-created, in the image of our true source and our true destiny.

"AMAZING GRACE"

The idea that we human beings are on a spiritual journey appears in numerous stories and traditions. One of these is the tradition of the pilgrim in the Russian Orthodox Church, which called those who desired holiness to take to the road, avoiding the comforts of the settled life in order to beg each day's food and shelter, relying on the sustenance that might come one's way by the grace of God. A recent church opera, *The Three Hermits,* with music by Stephen Paulus and libretto by Michael Dennis Browne, sets the prayer of such a pilgrim to music. The arrangement of the "Pilgrim's Hymn" is in a four-part vocal setting that is hauntingly mysterious and strong.

> Even before we call on Your name to ask You, O God,
> When we seek for the words to glorify You, You hear
>   our prayer;

In this music we hear the paradox once again of a divine hearing of our very human struggle to form words of prayer. The hymn continues:

> Unceasing love, O unceasing love, surpassing all we
>   know.
> Glory to the Father, and to the Son, and to the Holy
>   Spirit.
> Even with darkness sealing us in, we breathe Your
>   name,
> And through all the days that follow so fast, we trust in
>   You;
> Endless Your grace, endless Your grace beyond all
>   mortal dream.
> Both now and forever, and unto ages and ages, Amen.

This fusion of words and exquisite lyrical music for chorus, which comes at the conclusion of the opera, gives a hint at what we mean by the search for God. It is clearly sung by one with a restless heart, one who is aware of living in darkness, seeking words with which to speak of ultimate things that surpass human knowing. And yet the paradox is plain: even though this pilgrim does not have the words and even before the pilgrim tries to find them, God is seeking the pilgrim. Even though the darkness is encompassing, this pilgrim has an ultimate orientation in life. These words of praise echo the humility and the vulnerability of our human pilgrimage as they depict humanity sounding praise before the source of unceasing love and endless grace, even in the midst of uncertainty and darkness.

As we have noticed before, the old hymn "Amazing Grace" seems to resonate with the experience of many spiritual seekers, including many who would reject its literal imagery of human wretchedness. Perhaps that is because it expresses a unique form of human joy: "I once was lost but now I'm found." Many human experiences might be described in this way; some people would say they have been found when good and true love finally comes to them, others when they return to sobriety after a long period of addiction. To call such experiences grace is to acknowledge that they come as gift; we may have spent years trying to make these things happen, but in the end they found us. For the two of us, these human experiences are clues to the mystery that goodness beyond ourselves—a goodness we name as being from God—is always seeking us.

An eighteenth-century version of Psalm 23 speaks of the comfort of being found in a beautiful verse often sung as a hymn (to an old tune from *Southern Harmony*, a collection of early American shape-note tunes first published in 1835):

The sure provisions of my God attend me all my days;
O may Your House be my abode, and all my work be
    praise.
There would I find a settled rest, while others go and
    come;
No more a stranger, or a guest, but like a child at home.

Yet this beautifully childlike image of being found by God's gracious hospitality can also come in rigorous adult form. One of those soundings in the face of some of the greatest darkness of the twentieth century exists in the hymn text of "By Gracious Powers" by the German theologian and pastor Dietrich Bonhoeffer, who was executed by the Nazis just days before the Allied victory in April 1945 for his role in resisting Hitler.

By gracious powers so wonderfully sheltered,
And confidently waiting, come what may,
We know that God is with us night and morning,
And never fails to greet us each new day.

Then comes the honest cry:

Yet is this heart by its old foe tormented,
Still evil days bring burdens hard to bear;
O give our frightened souls the sure salvation
For which, O Lord, you taught us to prepare.
And when this cup you give is filled to brimming
With bitter sorrow, hard to understand
we shall remember all the days we lived through,
and our whole life shall then be yours alone.

Whether in lament or in praise, whether in the comfort of our childhood home or when great things are required of us as adults, the great surprise is that music can be there to soothe or to stir our spirits in the search for God and to open us to notice God's search for us. When just the music our spirits need finally finds us, it carries with it a sense that overwhelming love and grace sustains our whole humanity.

We human beings cannot live the fullness intended for us without music that sounds the heights and depths of the mystery of the world. For us (Emily and Don), working our Saturday night and Sunday morning venues, we listen for music that can take us from time to time into the depths of our humanity and into the mystery of the divine energies at work in the world. Religious communities do well to listen for humanity's hopes and fears, its joys and sorrows in music, great and small, not only within their communities but also beyond them. Popular music would do well to resist simple formulas and commercial exploitation and to encourage the flourishing of fresh poetry and vital rhythms. All music—jazz and classical, secular and sacred—needs to draw inspiration from honest encounters with the mysteries of life. We are all passing in time and all in a vast human pilgrimage.

Human beings cannot do without such soundings of earth and heaven. In a time when music is often reduced to advertising jingles, those who listen in churches or synagogues and in bars or concert halls need life-giving alternatives. In the aftermath of a century in which triumphalist human regimes have used music for nationalist and racist purposes, we need music that reveals ways of justice and freedom. In a time when religious communities often settle for too little, we need the ancient full stretch of praise, lament, wonder, and hope, of truth and grateful openness to the divine.

The French writer and mystic Simone Weil wrote of how we most often obtain what is most precious not by aggressively going out in search of it but by waiting with attentiveness. The two of us believe that if we practice attentiveness with open ears and open hearts, we may hear the divine voice calling to us through music, on Saturday night as well as Sunday morning. Our experience as musicians has allowed us to hear this voice from time to time. Listening in this way, we also hear the cries and whispers of suffering and the protests of the justice bearers. In this listening, music is never a distraction from the real, whether for worshipers, concertgoers, or rock fans. Rather, it opens us to what is most real in humanity's suffering and glory, and in the mystery of the God who is searching for us, a source of life and hope deeper than we can conceive.

Listen, and sing. When you find yourselves being found by the music, tell a friend. Begin with the music you already cherish but live with openness to the possibility that in the coming years music you have not yet heard will lead you more deeply into the mystery at the heart of all that is. We wish you joy and courage as you discover your songlines and as you learn to sing new songs as well. May music be a wellspring from which you will drink courage and joy. If you awaken to the search for God, may you hear in some unexpected music that God is seeking you. May you listen and sing in ways that build up your own life and the shared life of humankind within this beautiful, terrifying, music-gifted world.

References

Whenever possible, hymn page references are from *The United Methodist Hymnal* (UMH) (Nashville, Tenn.: United Methodist Publishing House, 1989). Historical background on the author and composer of each text and tune in this hymnal can be found in *Companion to the United Methodist Hymnal* (Nashville, Tenn.: Abingdon Press, 1993).

Unless otherwise noted, the African American spirituals we quote are in the public domain, including "Sometimes I Feel like a Motherless Chile" and "Let Us Break Bread Together."

The quoted lyrics from songs by the Indigo Girls appear with the permission of Amy Ray and Emily Saliers and Sony Music.

Unless otherwise indicated, Scripture quotations are from the New Revised Standard Version.

PREFACE

"The shattering experience of music" is from Abraham Joshua Heschel's 1957 essay "The Vocation of the Cantor" in *The Insecurity of Freedom: Essays on Human Existence* (New York: Schocken Books, 1966), p. 246.

CHAPTER ONE

The image of songlines was popularized by the late British fiction writer Bruce Chatwin in *The Songlines* (London: Jonathan Cape, 1987). He imagined that children of certain Aboriginal peoples in Australia receive a songline at birth. Such songlines were said to trace pathways that could be "walked as liturgies, generation upon generation," giving knowledge of land and life. "All the freaky people make the beauty of the world" is from "Stay Human," a song by Michael Franti, lead musician in the band Spearhead. The African American spiritual "Let Us Break Bread Together" (#618 UMH) draws on a New Testament depiction of worship in the early church, a pattern still present in many communities around the world: "They devoted themselves to the apostles' teaching and fellowship, to the breaking of bread and the prayers" (Acts 2:42).

The seraphim chanted to one another, "Holy, holy, holy, is the Lord of hosts; the whole earth is full of his glory," in Isaiah's vision in the temple (6:1–3). The text of "Holy, Holy, Holy! Lord God Almighty" (#64 UMH), by Reginald Heber (1783–1826), echoes their song. Violeta Parra (1917–1967), poet and musician, traveled throughout Chile collecting her people's folk songs. "*Gracias a la Vida*" is her best-known and most often recorded original song. Paul Marechal is quoted from *Dancing Madly Backwards: A Journey into God* (New York: Crossroad, 1982), p. 7.

CHAPTER TWO

See F. E. Hutchinson's book *The Complete Works of George Herbert* (Oxford: Clarendon, 1941) for "Prayer I" from *The Temple* (1633). Mark Burrows granted permission to publish his reflections as his brother, John, struggled for life. Fritjof Capra describes the cosmic dance of Shiva in *The Tao of Physics* (Boston: Shambhala, 1999), pp. 225–246. This story from India about creation being danced into life is told in "Music," the chapter Don and Emily wrote with Mark Winstanley and Liz Marshburn for *Way to Live: Christian Practices for Teens,* edited by Dorothy C. Bass and Don C. Richter (Nashville, Tenn.: Upper Room Books, 2002), p. 270. The later story of the family whose father suffered from Alzheimer's is also drawn from *Way to Live,* p. 267. Don has explored the importance of the senses to music and worship more extensively in *Worship Come to Its Senses* (Nashville, Tenn.: Abingdon Press, 1996).

The text of the best-known hymn by Folliot Sanford Pierpoint (1835–1917), "For the Beauty of the Earth" (#92 UMH), is traditionally set to the tune known as *"Treuer Heiland"* (True Savior) or "Dix," by William Dix (1837–1898). The text is in the public domain. Augustine's testimony or spiritual autobiography, *Confessions,* is available in many editions; see Book 10, 6:8 and Book 9, 4:8. The quotation from Suzanne Langer is from *Philosophy in a New Key* (Cambridge, Mass.: Harvard University Press, 1942), p. 206. The text "When in Our Music God Is Glorified" (#68 UMH), by Fred Pratt Green (1903–2001), quoted here and at the close of Chapter Four, was commissioned in 1971 for *A Festival of Praise* (Carol Stream, Ill.: Hope, 1972).

References

Chapter Three

The quotes in the first paragraph are from Emily's song "Virginia Woolf." Robert Lowry (1822–1899) wrote both text and tune of "My Life Flows on in Endless Song" published as hymn #781 in *With One Voice: A Lutheran Resource for Worship* (Minneapolis: Augsburg, 1995). Inspired by a trip to Palestine, Phillips Brooks (1835–1893) wrote "O Little Town of Bethlehem" (#230 UMH) in 1868 while serving as pastor at Holy Trinity Church in Philadelphia. Benjamin Britten composed *War Requiem* (London: Boosey & Hawkes) in 1962, using Wilfred Owen's poems as text. The line "half the seed of Europe, one by one" is from Owen's poem "The Parable of the Old Man and the Young," written shortly before his death in the closing days of World War I. It can be found in *The Collected Poems of Wilfred Owen,* edited by Cecil Day Lewis (London: Chatto & Windus, 1946). The film *Casablanca* was produced in 1943 by Hal B. Wallis. Kurt Weill (1900–1950) fled Nazi Germany in 1935 and came to the United States, where he met Maxwell Anderson (1888–1959). Their collaboration, "September Song"—Weill's tune and Anderson's text—was first performed in the 1938 musical *Knickerbocker Holiday*.

Chapter Four

David Abram writes about the purely oral culture in *The Spell of the Sensuous* (New York: Vintage Books, 1996), p. 140. The quotation about "the congregational voice" is from Alice Parker's book *Melodious Accord: Good Singing in Church* (Chicago: Liturgy Training, 1991), p. 7.

R. S. Thomas (1913–2000), whom many consider the preeminent Welsh poet writing in English, published "Evening" in the volume *No Truce with the Furies* (Newcastle-upon-Tyne, England: Bloodaxe Books, 1995), p. 19. "Finlandia" is the name of the tune by Jean Sibelius (1865–1957) to which Lloyd Stone (1912–1992) set his text "This Is My Song" (#437 UMH). Jaroslav Vajda (b. 1919) writes that the inspiration for "Now the Silence" (1968; #619 UMH) came while he was shaving. He calls it a hymn without rhyme or "worn clichés" that relies entirely on "rhythm and repetition to be singable." Carl Schalk (b. 1929), a frequent collaborator with Vajda, wrote the tune "NOW" for this text a year later. See Mary Kay Stulken, *Hymnal Companion to the Lutheran Book of Worship* (Philadelphia: Fortress Press, 1981), pp. 286–287.

On matching ourselves to the music's feeling, see Thomas Clifton, *Music as Heard: A Study in Applied Phenomenology* (New Haven, Conn.: Yale University Press, 1983), p. 295. Mary Mothersill writes about each person and some works of art having a soul in *Beauty Restored* (Oxford: Clarendon Press, 1984), p. 423. "Amazing Grace" (#378 UMH) was written by John Newton in 1779.

"How often making music we have found a new dimension in the world of sound" is from Fred Pratt Green's "When in Our Music God Is Glorified" (#68 UMH).

Chapter Five

Melva Costen chaired the Presbyterian Church (USA) Hymnal Committee that produced the *Presbyterian Hymnal* (Louisville, Ky.: Westminster/John Knox, 1990).

"Whatever people can say with passion . . ." comes from

Don's essay "Singing Our Lives" in *Practicing Our Faith: A Way of Life for a Searching People* (San Francisco: Jossey-Bass, 1997), p. 182. *"Cuando el Pobre"* (#434 UMH) by J. A. Olivar and Miguel Manzano draws its images from the parable of the sheep and the goats in which Jesus says, "Truly I tell you, just as you did it to one of the least of these who are members of my family, you did it to me" (see Matthew 25:31–46).

CHAPTER SIX

Tom Troeger's story is from page 11 of *Trouble at the Table: Gathering the Tribes for Worship* (Nashville, Tenn.: Abingdon Press, 1992), which he wrote with Carol Doran. Special thanks go to BeSean Jackson, a graduate student in theological studies at Emory University, who shared his remarks in a faculty-student discussion. The Thomas G. Long quotation is from his book *Beyond the Worship Wars: Building Vital and Faithful Worship* (Bethesda, Md.: Alban Institute, 2001), p. 2. "What language shall I borrow" is from the third stanza of "O Sacred Head, Now Wounded" (#286 UMH), a Latin text translated by Paul Gerhardt (1607–1676) and long wedded to the work known as the "Passion Chorale," written by Hans L. Hassler (1564–1612).

CHAPTER SEVEN

The text to "O God, Our Help in Ages Past" (#117 UMH), written by Isaac Watts (1674–1748), is a metric rendition of

Psalm 90: "Lord, you have been our dwelling place in all generations."

William Harvey's story is from Barry Green's book *The Mastery of Music* (New York: Random House, 2003), pp. 279–280. The quotation beginning with "A hammering anxiety" is taken from *Upheavals of Thought: The Intelligence of the Emotions* by Martha Nussbaum (New York: Cambridge University Press, 2001), p. 283. "He Never Said a Mumbalin' Word" is hymn #291 in the UMH. The poem "Strange Fruit" was written by "Lewis Allan" (Abel Meeropol, 1903–1986), who was haunted by a photograph of the 1930 lynching of Thomas Shipp and Abram Smith in Marion, Indiana.

The story about Luisa is from George Dennison's *"Luisa Domic"* and *"Shawno"* (Hanover, N.H.: Steerforth Press, 1994), pp. 80–82. "When Pain and Terror Strike by Chance," text by Brian Wren, appears in *New Beginnings* (Carol Stream, Ill.: Hope, 1993, song #11).

CHAPTER EIGHT

Lee Hayes and Pete Seeger wrote the words and music of "If I Had a Hammer," also known as "The Hammer Song" (Tro-Ludlow Music, Inc./BMI, copyright © 1958, 1962).

Gurney Norman's story is taken from *Voices from the Mountains,* collected and recorded by Guy and Candie Carawan (Athens: University of Georgia Press, 1966, 1975), p. 63. (To obtain further information on the Carawans' publications and music, go to http://photo.ucr.edu/projects/carawan/resources.html.)

Sarah Ogan Gunning (1910–1983), the Appalachian folksinger who later performed in Carnegie Hall, set her protest songs to familiar old tunes, often with an ironic twist. She modeled the song quoted here on the traditional "Precious Memories" and titled it "Dreadful Memories."

Nimrod Workman's song is featured in *Voices from the Mountains,* pp. 156–157.

The 1992 CD of *Sing for Freedom: The Story of the Civil Rights Movement Through Its Songs* (Smithsonian/Folkways) contains useful liner notes. Don interviewed Guy and Candie Carawan in April 2004 at the Art and Social Change conference at Emory University in Atlanta. Their personal reflections are printed here with their permission.

Joshua Dunson's reflections on the 1964 civil rights gathering in Atlanta are from his memoirs *Freedom in the Air* (New York: International Publishers, 1965), p. 101.

"The Voice of God Is Calling" (#436 UMH) by John Haynes Holmes refers to the call of the prophet Isaiah. God asks, "Whom shall I send? Who will go for us?" Isaiah responds "Here I am; send me!" (Isaiah 6:8). "O God of Earth and Altar" (#428 in *The Lutheran Book of Worship,* Minneapolis: Augsburg, 1978) by the English poet Gilbert Chesterton (1874–1936) is most often sung to the English folk tune "King's Lynn." "What Does the Lord Require?" based on Micah 6:8, is hymn #441 in the UMH.

Brian Wren's text "Arise, Shine Out, Your Light Has Come" (#725 UMH) draws its prophetic power from the poetic vision of Isaiah 60:1–3, who sings hope to the people of Jerusalem. John Bell's song "The Summons" was first published in *Heaven Shall Not Wait* (Iona Community, Scotland: Wild Goose, 1987). Fred Pratt Green, who along with Brian Wren and Fred Kahn was part of what has been called the New English Hymnody Renaissance of the late 1960s and 1970s, wrote "When the Church of Jesus Shuts Its Outer Door" (#592 UMH).

CHAPTER NINE

"Let Us Break Bread Together" (#618 UMH) originally served as a gathering song for eighteenth-century slaves in Virginia who were meeting secretly to plan their escape. The song signaled the time and place of the meeting. After the Civil War, the first two stanzas of the spiritual as we find it in most hymnbooks were added, making this a song for Holy Communion. "O Sacred Head Now Wounded" is hymn #286 in the UMH. Richard Mant (1776–1848), poet and priest in the Church of England, wrote "For All the Saints, Who from Their Labors Rest" (#555 UMH). Huub Oosterhuis set his text "What Is This Place" to the 1626 Dutch tune *"Komt Nu met Zang"* (Come Now with Singing), the first hymn featured in *Hymnal: A Worship Book* (Scottsdale, Pa.: Mennonite Publishing House, 1992).

CHAPTER TEN

Although Abraham Joshua Heschel's book carries the outdated title *Man's Quest for God: Studies in Prayer and Symbolism* (New York: Scribner, 1954), it continues to bear truth about prayer to contemporary readers. His observations about "the sense of the ineffable" and regaining "a sense of mystery" are on pp. 50 and 139, respectively. Further quotes from Heschel are from *The Insecurity of Freedom,* pp. 246 and 248. Anne Lamott is quoted from her book *Traveling Mercies: Some Thoughts on Faith* (New York: Pantheon Books, 1999), pp. 46–48.

Christina Rossetti wrote the text and Gustav Holst the tune for "In the Bleak Midwinter" (#221 UMH). Charles Wesley's 1747 hymn "Love Divine, All Loves Excelling" is #384 in the UMH.

A recording of the "Pilgrim's Hymn" from the opera *The Three Hermits* is on the 1997 CD recording *D'Note Classics,* with the Motet Choir of House of Hope Presbyterian Church, conducted by Thomas Lancaster.

"My Shepherd Will Supply My Need," based on Psalm 23, is set to the Southern Harmony tune *Resignation* (#172 in the *Presbyterian Hymnal*).

Dietrich Bonhoeffer's hymn "By Gracious Powers" (#517 UMH) was translated from the German by Fred Pratt Green and set to a tune by Charles Hubert Hasting Parry called "Intercessor," written in 1904.

The Authors

DON SALIERS teaches at Emory University, where he is the William R. Cannon Distinguished Professor of Theology and Worship. An active church musician and worship leader, he has been the organist and choirmaster at Cannon Chapel for nearly thirty years.

EMILY SALIERS is a singer-songwriter, best known as half of the Grammy Award–winning Indigo Girls, whose career spans twenty years. She and Amy Ray have performed throughout the Americas and around the world.

Index

of, art shaped by, 16–18; revising, debate over, 107–109; seasons and holy days within, living by the rhythm of, 49–50; social vision of, 145; sound of, 19, 21. *See also specific traditions*

Christmas songs, 9, 44, 45–46, 49, 91, 175

Church bells, 19

Civil rights movement, 4, 133, 134, 138–143

Clashes, cultural, 103–104

Classical Brubeck (Brubeck), 156

Classical music: crossing over from, 156, 158, 159; disturbed by, 99; early exposure to, 5, 9, 11; and melody, 63; and the restless heart, 171; sounds present in both popular and, 164; use of, in commercials, 105, 106. *See also specific songs and composers*

Classical polyphony, allowing, 161

Clichés, 16, 17, 149, 155, 163, 165

Clifton, T., 72

Clockwork Orange, A, 105

"Closer to Fine" (Saliers), 59

Coal mining, injustice of, 136–137

Cole, N. K., 80

Coltrane, J., 113

"Come Sunday" (Ellington), 101

Comfort zones, pushing beyond, 146

Commercial jingles, 106, 180

Commercialization, 85, 149, 180

Commercials, 105, 106–107, 180

Communal singing, 3, 34–35, 57, 82, 84, 155

Communion, 70–71, 170

Communion song, 13, 157

Communities: belonging to, 87–88; discovering, 75–76; disparate, gaps between, bridging, 86; expanding, 83; forming, 83; of hope, 89–95; of musical practice, 33–35

Complexity of souls and music, 72–73

Complicity, singing truth about, in injustice, 147

Confessions (Augustine), 31–32, 171

Consolation songs, 117, 128

Contrition, inducing sense of, 174

Coping, ways of, 126

Coppola, F. F., 106

1 Corinthians 13:1, 112

Costen, M., 82

Counterpoint, 64

Country music, 53–54, 90, 99, 104, 113, 127

Courage and joy, 181

Creation, 30, 176

Crossing back, 156–160

Crossing over, 11, 12, 78–79, 89, 95, 114, 147, 153–167

Crossover border/boundaries, 89, 160–167

Crueger, J., 159

Cruel use of music, 105–106

"Cuando el Pobre," 88–89, 147

Cuban music, 85, 148

Cultural clashes, 103–104

Cultural identity, 77, 98

Cultural understanding, opening up to, 104–105

Culture, hectic, taking time for music in, 43–44, 58

D

Dance music, 8, 49

Dancing, cosmic, 30–31

Dancing creation, 30

Dancing Madly Backwards (Marechal), 16

Das Lied von der Erde (Mahler), 17

Davis, M., 8, 77

Davis, S., Jr., 80

Day, D., 80

Hassler, H. L., 159

"He Never Said a Mumbalin' Word," 126

Healing: music's power of, 3, 127–131; preparing the way for, 174; process of, beginning, 118, 119, 121–122

Hearing, aspects of, 55–74. *See also* Listening

Heart metaphor, 24

Heart (the band), 87

Heartache, music about, 53–54

Heartbeats, rhythm of, 22, 23–24, 28, 62

Hearts, restless, music calling to, 171–176, 177

Heavy metal music, 100, 158

Heblett, C., 143

Hectic culture, taking time for music in, 43–44, 58

Hendrix, J., 100

Herbert, G., 24–25

Heschel, A. J., 170–171, 174

Highlander Folk Center, 134, 140

Hillbilly Hit Parade, 136

Hindu tradition, sound of, 20

Hip-hop, 63, 104, 113, 158

Hispanic music, 88–89, 147

"History of Us" (Saliers), 51–52

Hitler, A., 106, 179

Holiday, B., 126

Holy Communion, 70–71

"Holy, Holy, Holy," 13

Holy Week, 49, 159

Honor the Earth tours, 149

Hope: communities of, 89–95; prayer of, 172; songs of, 131, 133, 143, 144

Hot Club of France Quintet, 10

"Hound Dog" (Presley), 100, 158

Houston, W., 87

"How Great Thou Art," 51, 109

Human suffering, awareness of, 17

Human truth, sources of, in touch with, 166

Humanity: journeying into depths of, 1–2, 18; listening for depth of, 180, 181; love for, 53, 93; metaphor for, 62

Hymns: commingling with speeches and prayers, 138–139; conflict over, 101, 107–109; crossing over to, 155, 158–159; emerging forms of, 164; during funerals, 117, 124; on God's search for us, 176, 177; on grace, 178–179; on language, 110; on life's endless song, 42; mixing lament and hope, 131; of mystic harmony, 31; older women recalling favorite, 51; of praise, 13, 37, 74; of the seasons, 49–50; silence in, 70–71; that carry social vision, 143–148; that make a difference, 152; using metaphor of the heart, 24; wider range of, bringing, into church, 85–86, 88–89

I

"I Come to the Garden Alone," 51

"I Have a Dream" (King), 150

"I Woke Up This Morning with My Mind Stayed on Freedom," 139

Icelandic songs, 60

Identities: cultural, 77; finding our, aspects of, 75–95; musical, 82–86, 88–89; sense of our, being threatened, 98. *See also* Personal identity

"If I Had a Hammer," 133

"I'll Be Home for Christmas," 91

Imagination, music tapping into, 59–60

Imagining love of God, 31–32

Imitation, learning through, 81, 87

Improvising, 11, 34, 81, 126

"Light Up a Lucky," 106
Lilith Fair tour, 113
Listening: for (and with) the soul, 16, 71–74; and appreciating silence, 66; attentive, 18, 55–56, 60–61, 112–113, 165, 181; for depth of humanity, 2, 180; to elements of music, practicing, 64–65; and hearing, aspects of, 55–74; importance of, 57–58, 110; with our whole selves, 58–61; willingness to engage in, 12, 111
Little Five Points Pub, 159
Lombardo, G., 8
London Symphony Orchestra, 156
Loneliness, 89, 90–91, 92, 115. *See also* Isolation and aloneness
Long, T., 107
Longings and reality, gap between, living in, 171
"Lord, Who Throughout These Forty Days," 49
Lord's Supper, 70–71
Lourdes, 63, 151
Love: of God, imagining, 31–32; and hope, songs of, 133; for humanity, 93; listening with, need for, 110; memories of, 48; and mortality, singing of, 52–53; of people and music, 81
"Love Divine, All Loves Excelling" (Wesley), 109, 176
Love songs, 44, 90, 158, 159
"Love Will Come to You," 92
Luisa Domic (Dennison), 128–129
Luke 1:46–53, 17
Luther, M., 109
Lynching, lament on, 126

M

Ma, Yo-Yo, 122, 158
Magnificat, 17
Mahler, G., 17, 55, 63, 73, 122

Making a difference, 148–152
Mandela, N., 138
Man's Quest for God (Heschel), 170–171
Marble Collegiate Church, 88
Marechal, P., 16
Marie, 26
Mass, Christian, 47–48, 60, 84, 161
Mass in B Minor (Bach), 159, 175
Mastery of Music, The (Green), 119–122
May, B., 80
McNair, S., 153
Media conglomerates, 149
Media reports, 108–109
Medieval Mass, 60
Meditation, 69
"Meditation," 121
Meeropol, A., 126
"Melodie" (Tchaikovsky), 121
Melodious Accord (Parker), 58
Melody, importance of, 34, 63
Memories, bringing back, 1, 9, 35, 46, 51, 76–77, 105. *See also* Remembering our lives
"Memory," 120
Memory, deep, requiring, 36
Mennonite music, 160
Mentors, 3
Messiah (Handel), 159
Metaphor: heart, 24; humanity, 62; shopping, 107; war, 107
Methodist church, 7–8, 10, 13–14
"Mighty Fortress Is Our God, A" (Luther), 109
Milhaud, D., 156
"Minute Waltz" (Chopin), 64
Mitchell, J., 46–47, 59, 60
Mood and emotions, evoking, 59, 63, 71–72
Moravian tradition, sound of, 21
Morehouse College Glee Club, 17
Morgan, R., 155
Mortality, 39, 40, 52–53, 127, 175
Mothersill, M., 72

Radio station ownership, issue of, 149

Rainey, W., 136

Raitt, B., 87

Rap music, 103–104, 158

Ravel, M., 59

Ray, A., 3, 26, 58, 68, 75, 80, 85, 93, 111, 123, 134, 148, 149, 157. *See also* Indigo Girls

Reagon, B., 140, 143

Reagon, C., 140, 143

Reality: connecting to larger, 29; encountering, 174, 175, 181; our longings and, gap between, living in, 171

Recording studios, constructing music in, aspects of, 61–62, 65

Re-creating ourselves, 1, 176

Reese, D., 140, 141, 142

"Rejoice in the Lamb" (Britten), 47

Remembering our lives, 33–37. *See also* Memories

Repentance, readiness for, 174

Resounding music, 29–33

Respect, 12, 112–114

Responsibilities: ethical, embracing, 134; human, one of the most important, 152

Restless hearts, music calling to, 171–176, 177

Revelation, 176

"Rhapsody in Blue" (Gershwin), 6

Rhythm: importance of, 34, 62–63; of our bodies, 21–29, 62; of the universe, 29–33; vital, encouraging, 180

"Ride of the Valkyries" (Wagner), 106

Riefenstahl, L., 106

Rite of Spring, The (Stravinsky), 62, 97–98, 100

Ritual, embodying, 33–37

Ritual songs, 33–34, 49

Robert Shaw Chorale, 151

Rock music, 99, 106, 107, 162

Rock 'n' roll, 63, 100, 158

"Rocky Mountain High" (Denver), 80

Roman Catholic tradition, 161

Ruach, 24

Ruechert, F., 122

Russia, Soviet, 84

Russian Orthodox Church, 176–177

S

Sacred and secular: crossing over between, aspects of, 153–167; determination of, questioning, 4–5

St. Andrew Presbyterian, 172–173

St. James Freewill Baptist Church, 101

St. John's Abbey Church, 19

St. John the Divine Cathedral, 101, 166

Saliers, D., book of, 83

Saliers, E., songs of, 50–51, 51–52, 59, 80, 93, 118, 123, 157

Saliers, H., 6–10, 155

Saliers, J., 49

Saturday night and Sunday morning, crossing over between, 5, 153–167

Sauter-Finegan band, 80

Schalk, C., 70

Schiller, F., 152

Schindler's List, 121

School systems, music programs being cut by, 93

Schubert, F., 63

Scotland community, 110

Scotland folk traditions, 145

Sea Island Singers, 140, 142

Searching for God, pathways in, aspects of, 169–181

Second Vatican Council, 161

Practicing Our Faith: A Way of Life for a Searching People

Dorothy C. Bass, editor

Paper

ISBN: 0–7879–3883–1

"As wise as grandparents, a good guide to living within our families and communities with integrity and generosity."—Kathleen Norris author of *Dakota* and *The Cloister Walk*

Many Christians are looking for ways to deepen their relationship with God by practicing their faith in everyday life. Some go on retreats but are often disappointed to find that the integrated life they experienced in a place apart is difficult to recreate in their day-to-day world. Many thoughtful, educated Christians search for spiritual guidance in Eastern religious traditions, unaware of the great riches within their own heritage.

To all these seekers, *Practicing Our Faith* offers help that is rooted in Christian faith and tradition. The contributors examine twelve central Christian practices—such as keeping Sabbath, honoring the body and forgiving one another—by placing each in historical and biblical context, reexamining relevance to our times, and showing how each gives depth and meaning to daily life. Shaped by the Christian community over the centuries yet richly grounded in the experiences of living communities today, these practices show us how Christian spiritual disciplines can become an integral part of how we live each day.

DOROTHY C. BASS is a noted church historian and director of the Valparaiso Project on the Education and Formation of People in Faith. She lives with her husband and children in Valparaiso, Indiana.

Receiving the Day: Christian Practices for Opening the Gift of Time

Dorothy C. Bass

Paper

ISBN: 0–7879–5647–3

"With wisdom, clarity, and sacred practicality, Dorothy C. Bass changes our relationship with Time. It needn't control us. Rather, the day, the week, and the year are each an opportunity for us to shape our lives in the peace and kindness of God. God's story becomes our story. This is a book of genuine insight and gentle leadership. Let it turn your calendar from a taskmaster into a gift from the Creator for creation and for you."

—Walter Wangerin Jr., author, *The Book of God*

"Those who struggle with pressures and limits of time—that is, all of us!—will find this book a rich resource to be tasted and tried. This deeply spiritual book dramatically reorients the heart of the reader . . . challenging our time-obsessed society and teaching the wisdom of religious practices."

—Bonnie J. Miller-McLemore, author, *And Also a Mother: Work and Family As Theological Dilemma*

"A profoundly useful book. . . . It reminds us forcibly that we are embodied creatures gifted by God with time too precious to fritter or work away. In its recommendations for healing our relationship to time it is often unsettlingly revolutionary, frequently subversive of our secular culture, and always full of Dorothy Bass's honest and generous reflections on her own life. It is a pleasure to recommend it."

—Roberta Bondi, author, *A Place to Pray: Reflections on the Lord's Prayer* and *Memories of God*

DOROTHY C. BASS, editor of *Practicing Our Faith* and a historian of American religion, is director of the Valparaiso University Project on the Education and Formation of People in Faith.

Testimony: Talking Ourselves into Being Christian

Thomas G. Long

Cloth

ISBN: 0–7879–6832–3

"Thomas G. Long has long been one of our most effective Christian talkers, and now in this trenchant testimony, the harvest of a rich and provoking ministry, he helps us all the better to talk about our Christian faith. Never have we had a greater need for authentic discourse, nor have we ever been better served."

—The Reverend Professor Peter J. Gomes, Plummer Professor of Christian Morals and Pusey Minister, Memorial Church, Harvard University

"In the rich vocabulary and cadence of his own speech, Thomas G. Long teaches us how to bring faith to speech in the everyday occurrences of life. One comes away from this book with an emboldened sense of how to speak of God in public places and spaces."

—Cleophus J. LaRue, Princeton Theological Seminary

In this groundbreaking book, Thomas G. Long—a theologian and respected authority on preaching—explores how Christians talk when they are not in church. Testimony breaks the stained-glass image of religious language to show how ordinary talking in our everyday lives—talk across the backyard fence, talk with our kids, talk about politics and the events of the day—can be sacred speech. In a world of spin, slick marketing, mindless chatter, and easy deceptions, Testimony shows that the hunger for truthful, meaningful, and compassionate speech is ultimately grounded in truth about God.

THOMAS G. LONG is Bandy Professor of Preaching, Candler School of Theology, Emory University. He is a former pastor and associate editor of the Journal for Preachers. Long is the author of fourteen books.